CAROLIN

Torben Betts

CAROLINE'S KITCHEN

OBERON BOOKS
LONDON

WWW.OBERONBOOKS.COM

First published as *Monogamy* in 2018

First published in 2019 by Oberon Books Ltd
521 Caledonian Road, London N7 9RH
Tel: +44 (0) 20 7607 3637 / Fax: +44 (0) 20 7607 3629
e-mail: info@oberonbooks.com
www.oberonbooks.com

PB ISBN: 9781786824110
E ISBN: 9781786824127

Cover image: Rebecca Pitt and Michael Wharley

Printed and bound by 4EDGE Limited, Hockley, Essex, UK.

for Alastair Whatley
Many thanks for your faith and support (once again)

Caroline's Kitchen was first performed as *Monogamy* at Malvern Theatre on 2nd May 2018 before embarking on a national tour. It had the following cast:

CAROLINE, Janie Dee

AMANDA, Genevieve Gaunt

GRAEME, Jack Sandle

LEO, Jack Archer

MIKE, Patrick Ryecart

SALLY, Charlie Brooks

The World Premiere took place at Park Theatre, London on 6th June 2018.

The play was then revised and retitled and opened at Derby Playhouse on 24th January 2019 before a second UK tour and taking part in the 2019 Brits-off-Broadway Festival. It had the following cast:

CAROLINE, Caroline Langrishe

AMANDA, Jasmyn Banks

GRAEME, James Sutton

LEO, Tom England

MIKE, Aden Gillett

SALLY, Elizabeth Boag

Creative Team:

Director Alastair Whatley
Design James Perkins
Lighting Chris Withers
Music And Sound Design Max Pappenheim
Associate Sound Design Richard Bell
Casting Ellie Collyer-Bristow CDG

Production Credits:

Producers Tom Hackney, Dom Hodson, Freddie Ryecart,
      Eilene Davidson
Assistant Producer Emily Altneu
Marketing Emma Martin
PR Amanda Malpass PR

Caroline's Kitchen was commissioned by The Original
Theatre Company and Ghostlight Theatre Productions.

Both productions were directed by Alastair Whatley.

Characters

CAROLINE
early-mid 50s

AMANDA
mid 20s

GRAEME
mid 30s/early 40s

LEO
early 20s

MIKE
early-mid 70s

SALLY
mid 30s/early 40s

two or three non-speaking roles

preferably to be played without an interval

A basement kitchen with the bar stools and also a large wooden dining table, around which chairs. Two exits: one to the garden area, the other to the hallway and the rest of the house. The kitchen has a window looking out onto the garden area. Visible are two bottles of champagne in ice buckets and a large crucifix, with a Christ attached, on the back wall. Late afternoon, midsummer's day. Oppressively hot. Possibly free-standing and/or handheld fans. Characters struggle with the heat throughout. CAROLINE stands centre stage, facing front. AMANDA waits in the kitchen area, large kitchen knife in hand.

CAROLINE: Hello, good morning and welcome to the very last in the current series of *Caroline's Kitchen* where as usual we are broadcasting live and where we'll be cooking up some delicious dishes with the help of a professional chef, a mystery celebrity, not to mention a member of the public who wants to share with you her absolute passion for…and here I kid you not…tripe.

CAROLINE walks over to the kitchen units.

But first let me introduce you to a young woman who started out life flipping burgers in her native Sweden before discovering her aptitude for all things culinary and eventually opening her own restaurant here in London. The Stockholm in Notting Hill, Ingrid Stephansson, has recently become Michelin-starred, I believe?

AMANDA: *(As Ingrid, convincing.)* That's right, Caroline. Last month we were awarded two stars.

CAROLINE: Golly. That's a lethal-looking weapon you're brandishing there?

AMANDA: This is a professional chef's knife made from Swedish steel and it shall be my gift to you.

CAROLINE: That's very generous.

AMANDA: You are more than welcome.

CAROLINE: Now in case you didn't realise, everyone, today is Midsummer's Day and for your compatriots, Ingrid, I believe it's a national holiday.

AMANDA: That is correct, Caroline.

CAROLINE: And so what will you be cooking up by way of celebration?

AMANDA: This morning I'll be showing you how to prepare my classic Swedish meatballs.

CAROLINE: Believe me, Ingrid's meatballs are a far cry from those you may have sampled at a certain Swedish furniture store.

AMANDA: And my meatballs will be accompanied by what we call *Janssons's Temptation* which is essentially a casserole made with grated potatoes, onion, anchovies and cream.

CAROLINE: I am salivating already.

AMANDA: And then, for dessert, I'll be making a delicious Swedish almond cheesecake with macerated strawberries and mint.

CAROLINE: Sounds divine.

AMANDA: And we're going to be washing all this down with some of this superb akvavit.

CAROLINE: Which is kind of like a fruit brandy?

AMANDA: So no doubt, Caroline, you'll be absolutely shit-faced by the end of the show.

GRAEME enters from the house.

GRAEME: Sorry. This a bad time?

CAROLINE: Don't worry, we were just…

AMANDA: *(As herself, her script now visible.)* Rehearsing.

CAROLINE: We were just rehearsing.

AMANDA: For tomorrow morning.

CAROLINE: For tomorrow morning, yes.

Two (if possible) stage crew, who are continually sharing a joke, are now dressing the kitchen for the live show, while CAROLINE begins preparing the family supper.

GRAEME: I'm sort of...all finished up there now.

CAROLINE: Amanda, thank you so much for all your hard work today but...

AMANDA: It has as ever been an absolute pleasure.

CAROLINE: ...you can get off home now as I've this supper to prepare so...

AMANDA: Killing the fatted calf, are you?

CAROLINE: So to speak, yes.

GRAEME: Was checking you still want me to...

CAROLINE: *(To the crew.)* Can you remember that I am actually using the kitchen tonight so someone'll need to clean it up first thing?

GRAEME: ...fix the door on Mike's room?

CAROLINE: *(To the crew.)* And I don't want those there tonight, if that's possible?

GRAEME: I mean, I can always come back next week if...

CAROLINE: No, if you could do that now please, Graeme?

GRAEME: No problem.

CAROLINE: *(As the crew leave the kitchen.)* Isn't there time to finish all this in the morning?!

The stage crew laugh, while AMANDA is alerted to her phone.

AMANDA: *Uno momento, por favor.*

AMANDA leaves for the garden, while CAROLINE is now busy preparing food.

GRAEME: Is there any chance we could have a quick chat or…?

The stage crew return and continue dressing the set, still laughing.

CAROLINE: Guys, can you please be very careful with that?

They watch the stage crew continue to dress the 'set'.

GRAEME: See the *For Sale* sign's finally up?

CAROLINE: This morning, yes.

GRAEME: Bet there'll be a stampede.

CAROLINE: *(To the stage crew.)* Could you leave that where it is, please?

A silence as GRAEME watches her.

GRAEME: Caroline?

CAROLINE: *(Busy with food prep.)* Hello there?

GRAEME: I was hoping that maybe you and me could…

CAROLINE: *(To the stage crew.)* Look, I really need you both to go home now!

They both stop in their tracks.

What I mean is…thank you. But all this can be done before we go live tomorrow, can't it?

They exit just as AMANDA returns, holding an iPad from which she rarely looks up. She continually wipes her nose with the back of her hand.

AMANDA: Seems tomorrow the perennially unemployable 1980s quiz show host is to be replaced by yet another pretty but essentially unremarkable actress from one of the hospital soaps.

CAROLINE: Say all that again?

GRAEME: Okay so... I might as well... You know, go fix that door and then... Well, that'll be that, I suppose.

GRAEME exits into the house.

AMANDA: She is apparently a loquacious little madame and quite *au fait* with this kind of thing.

Knock/rings on the front door.

Now that might well be Mrs Minto.

CAROLINE: Who's Mrs Minto?

AMANDA: Coming she is to survey thy humble abode.

CAROLINE: Already?

AMANDA: Estate agent called not twenty minutes ago.

CAROLINE: But I really can't have anyone coming *now*.

AMANDA: It'll all be tickety-boo.

CAROLINE: We're having a family gathering tonight.

AMANDA: She's a cash buyer apparently and desperate for a speedy purchase.

CAROLINE: Amanda, I expressly told you I didn't want anyone coming until Monday.

More knocks/rings.

Oh, for goodness' sake.

CAROLINE exits to the house.

AMANDA's phone goes to her ear.

AMANDA: Hi, babes? *(A sudden mood change.)* What you talking about? But we arranged this *weeks ago*, Dominic! I don't care that she's your wife, do I? You promised me!

You promised me you'd be spending this weekend with *me*!

The call is over and she battles her upset.

CAROLINE: *(Entering.)* …because we weren't expecting you till twenty past?

LEO: *(Entering.)* I caught an earlier train.

CAROLINE: Well, come in, come in…

LEO: Thank you.

AMANDA: *(Brave face.)* Hold on a moment, my lovely, as reception down here runs the whole gamut from appalling to completely non-existent.

She exits to the garden.

CAROLINE: Can I get you anything?

LEO: I'm alright, ta.

CAROLINE: We've got champagne in for later.

LEO: You know I'm not a drinker so…

CAROLINE: Yes, but I thought tonight you might possibly make an exception?

LEO: It's absurdly hot today.

CAROLINE: It is.

LEO: They're dropping like flies out there. At least two people fainted on the Underground just now.

CAROLINE: Oh dear.

LEO: Party's well and truly over, isn't it?

CAROLINE: What party, sorry?

LEO: The end of the world is nigh et cetera.

CAROLINE: Is it?

LEO: Of course.

He examines the wine bottle on the table.

Anyway...I thought you were giving up?

CAROLINE: It's actually quite hard. You know, with the show. We get so much free booze, and good-quality booze as well. And it's sort of all part of the deal, really.

LEO: Eat, drink and be merry?

CAROLINE: Something like that.

LEO: For tomorrow we die.

A silence.

Do I detect the unmistakable stench of slow-roasting cow flesh?

CAROLINE: Thought I'd cook up something nice for us.

LEO: Although you know I'm a vegan?

CAROLINE: Oh, you still are, are you?

LEO: I still am.

CAROLINE: So is there any way you could sort of *not* be one? I mean, just for tonight?

LEO: What you don't realise is that unless everyone on the planet stops consuming animal products as of right this moment then global warming's going to wipe out the whole...

CAROLINE: I can't hear this again.

LEO: The inconvenient truth.

CAROLINE: So what shall I feed you then?

LEO: You tell me, you're the chef.

A silence.

So where's Mike?

CAROLINE: You mean, where's your father?

LEO: That's the chap.

CAROLINE: Playing golf.

LEO: Say it isn't so!

CAROLINE: He'll be back any minute.

A silence.

Well, I might… If you don't mind.

LEO: You go ahead. It's your liver.

She drinks and continues with the food prep. He sits. A silence.

So come on then. I've been on tenterhooks.

CAROLINE: What about?

LEO: You know perfectly well what about.

CAROLINE: I'm not sure I do.

LEO: How did he take it?

CAROLINE: How did he take what?

LEO: You know what.

CAROLINE: I don't know what.

LEO: Don't tell me you haven't told him?

CAROLINE: Told who?

LEO: Told Dad?

CAROLINE: Told Dad what?

LEO: Are you serious?

CAROLINE: That man is such a worry to me.

LEO: Did he have the heart attack you assured me he'd have?

CAROLINE: He really doesn't like growing old.

LEO: Or did he take it like a twenty-first century man?

CAROLINE: I mean, he *really* doesn't like it.

LEO: But I do need you to tell me that you've told him.

AMANDA back on from the garden.

AMANDA: Now, lovely, I've some good news and some bad news. Which you want first?

CAROLINE: *(To LEO.)* We can talk about this later…

AMANDA: Always prefer the bad news first myself. Get the bad news out of the way is what I always say. Swallow the bad news first, take it on the chin and then after that the only way is up sort of thing.

LEO: When though?

CAROLINE: So what *is* the bad news?

AMANDA: If you have the good news first then it might not be as good as you expect and then when the bad news follows on from that…

LEO: I was actually hoping you and I could sit down together and…?

CAROLINE: Please tell me whichever you…

AMANDA: The bad news is that the *Mail on Sunday* have somehow got hold of some mildly embarrassing photographs of you and, despite my most earnest endeavours, they say they will definitely be publishing them the day after tomorrow.

LEO: Mum?

AMANDA: But the good news is I've just seen them and, as I say, they're actually not that bad.

LEO: Because I really need us to talk about this before…

AMANDA: I mean, they're bad but they're not, I don't think, career-endingly bad.

CAROLINE: Career-endingly?

AMANDA: But the bottom line is you really need to start thinking about confining your nights out to…

CAROLINE: To what?

AMANDA: Well, to nights in.

CAROLINE: Nights in?

AMANDA: Might be for the best.

CAROLINE: Can I see them?

AMANDA: It'll be a tiny bit humiliating for a day or so but then I'm certain it'll quickly blow over.

AMANDA hands CAROLINE her iPad.

CAROLINE: Are you sure that's me?

AMANDA: This would appear to be the case.

CAROLINE: But it could be anyone!

AMANDA: This is a much better one.

CAROLINE: I look about ninety!

AMANDA: Don't let it get to you.

CAROLINE: It *is* getting to me.

AMANDA: Then try not to let it.

LEO: What's going on?

CAROLINE: I really don't want to swear but…

AMANDA: *(To LEO.)* Heaven forfend that she would!

CAROLINE: To think there are people out there who actually masquerade as human beings who make a living taking photographs of innocent people who have done nothing wrong other than enjoy a night out with friends and…

AMANDA: You need to blame the people who buy the paper.

LEO: *She* buys the paper.

CAROLINE: I do not!

AMANDA: You must be the oft-boasted-about Leo?

LEO: She's been reading it all her life.

CAROLINE: I've been reading the *Guardian* for ages now!

LEO: Which is equally vile.

CAROLINE: In what way?

LEO: But for slightly different reasons.

AMANDA: Yes, it really is a den of iniquity, my lovely, out here in the real world.

LEO: Is it?

AMANDA: Which you'll no doubt soon be discovering for yourself now you've been unceremoniously shat out of the closeted world of academia.

LEO: I'm sorry?

CAROLINE: It looks like I've been punched in the face.

LEO: *(To CAROLINE.)* Did she really just say that?

AMANDA: You maybe don't look your best but…

CAROLINE: These people, Leo, they actually hide in the bushes in the front garden…

AMANDA: This, my lovely, is the price of fame.

LEO: She's not *that* famous, is she?

CAROLINE: I've never done any harm to anyone and I'm having a little night out with friends and I get a cab back home and as I get out I stumble and fall onto the pavement and then some odious little paparazzi, instead of helping me to my feet like any decent human being would do, he takes all these nasty photos of me and suddenly, what, suddenly I'm front page news?!

AMANDA: *(To LEO.)* I doubt she'll be front page.

LEO: Can I see?

CAROLINE: I really don't think there's any need for him to...

AMANDA takes the iPad off CAROLINE and hands it to him.

AMANDA: I'm Amanda by the way. I look after your mum.

CAROLINE: For now.

AMANDA: And forever.

LEO: Nice to meet you.

AMANDA: And I understand heartfelt congratulations are in order?

LEO: I think.

AMANDA: Not every day you get a degree from Oxford, is it?

LEO: Cambridge.

CAROLINE: He got a First.

AMANDA: I think, my lovely, you might have mentioned that before!

CAROLINE: Have I?

AMANDA: Maybe once or twice?

LEO: What happened to that other girl?

CAROLINE: She's on maternity leave.

LEO: Right.

CAROLINE: Unfortunately.

AMANDA: Unfortunately?

LEO: How drunk *were* you?

AMANDA: As you can see she does look a tad bleary-eyed…

CAROLINE: Hardly at all.

LEO: This *is* pretty awful.

CAROLINE: I know, I know…

AMANDA: But show me the person who says they've not fallen out of a cab blind-drunk at half three in the morning and I'll show you…

LEO: *I* haven't.

AMANDA: …a bare-faced liar.

CAROLINE: Can't you call the paper again?

AMANDA: The thing is to affect nonchalance.

CAROLINE: Nonchalance?

AMANDA: Nonchalance is sort of like…

CAROLINE: I know what the word *means*, Amanda…

AMANDA: Anyway it may only appear in their online version.

CAROLINE: What terrible crime have I committed?

AMANDA: And no-one bothers much with that.

LEO: Well, you do present yourself as the darling of Middle England.

CAROLINE: Do I?

LEO: The perfect woman, with the perfect life and the perfect marriage, in the perfect house, with the perfect friends…

AMANDA: And now of course the perfect son is back on the scene…

CAROLINE: I really don't know what either of you are…

AMANDA: We need to calm down and look at all this with some measure of perspective.

CAROLINE: That's easy for you to say.

LEO: Maybe it's a wake-up call.

CAROLINE: In what way?

LEO: I think you're maybe…

CAROLINE: Maybe what?

LEO: …drinking too much.

AMANDA: Oucheroo!

CAROLINE: I'm sorry?

AMANDA: Now don't forget that Mrs Minto will be here shortly to…

CAROLINE: This is absolutely the *last* thing I need!

From here on in CAROLINE is prepping food.

AMANDA: But fret ye not for your friendly neighbourhood Amanda shall deal with her.

She exits to the garden, phone to ear.

LEO: Where did you find *her*?

CAROLINE: She's been foisted upon me by of one of the producers.

LEO: Seems completely…

CAROLINE: With whom she is clearly having some sort of…

LEO: …deranged.

CAROLINE: …affair.

LEO: The way she speaks to you…

CAROLINE: Married he is with three children under seven.

LEO: And I would humbly suggest…

CAROLINE: She knows I don't approve…

LEO: …she is using performance-enhancing…

CAROLINE: …which is why I suspect she has this…

LEO: … drugs of some description.

CAROLINE: …extremely snippy attitude towards me.

LEO: And who is Mrs Minto?

CAROLINE looks at the photos on the iPad.

CAROLINE: Look at me here.

LEO: So you haven't actually told him yet?

CAROLINE: This is all so…

LEO: Mum?

CAROLINE: …humiliating.

LEO: It's okay.

CAROLINE: I never asked for any of this. It's a silly television show, that's all. Why would anyone be interested in me? I'm just a boring, middle-class…

LEO: ….right-wing…

CAROLINE: I'm not at all right wing!

LEO: Can we please go somewhere where I can have your complete and undivided attention?

CAROLINE: You have my complete and undivided attention now.

LEO: Really?

CAROLINE: This is just so cruel.

LEO: Are you listening?

CAROLINE: Of course.

LEO: I'm not altogether sure that you are.

CAROLINE: Of course I'm listening.

LEO: You seem very…

CAROLINE: Oh God in heaven!

LEO: …distracted.

CAROLINE: And look at me here!

LEO: Mum, please!

CAROLINE: I'm so desperately sorry about this.

She drinks.

LEO: I need to tell you something!

CAROLINE: Anything, anything…

He watches her as she tidies away.

LEO: I've had my heart completely broken.

CAROLINE: Golly, who by?

LEO: What do you mean, who by?

CAROLINE: Not by that Japanese girl?

LEO: What Japanese girl?

CAROLINE: Iwo-Jima?

LEO: Iwo-Jima?

CAROLINE: I didn't know you were still seeing her?

LEO: I think you may be getting confused.

CAROLINE: Really?

LEO: Iwo-Jima is the island the Americans took from the
Japanese in 1945…

CAROLINE: Of course it is.

LEO: My friend's name is Ji-Woo.

CAROLINE: Anyway, the Japanese girl.

LEO: South Korean.

CAROLINE: South Korean, yes.

LEO: And you know I was never 'seeing' her. She was only
ever a….

CAROLINE: You see, we always thought you were…

LEO: Fucking her?

CAROLINE: For want of a more charming expression.

LEO: Well, I'm afraid I wasn't. You know *full well* that I wasn't.

CAROLINE: We really are so proud of you.

LEO: Why are you asking me this?

CAROLINE: So how did your friends do?

LEO: My friends?

CAROLINE: Yes…your friends?

LEO: Which friends are these?

CAROLINE: Your friends. At Cambridge?

LEO: Any friend in particular?

CAROLINE: I don't know. Tom? Jerry?

LEO: I have no friends called Tom and Jerry.

CAROLINE: What about the chap? You know, the one with
the ludicrous hair.

LEO: Nathan?

CAROLINE: That's him.

LEO: He dropped out after our first year.

CAROLINE: Did he really?

LEO: He really, really did.

CAROLINE: I can't believe they would actually take photographs, Leo!

LEO: Mum?

CAROLINE: Yes?

LEO: Why are you asking me about Ji-Woo?

CAROLINE: I'm sorry, it's just this piece of news has rather thrown me and…

LEO: Why are you still asking me about my relationships with…?

AMANDA re-enters from the garden.

AMANDA: The good news, Caroline, is that it's only gonna be in the online version.

CAROLINE: Yes because all I actually did was fall!

LEO: Mum?

AMANDA: Do we think it's a capital crime to be a fifty -something woman and be…

LEO: Because I *will* tell him if…

AMANDA: …a little bit slaughtered at three o'clock in the morning?

CAROLINE: I really wasn't so…

AMANDA: No, my lovely, we most certainly do not!

CAROLINE: …slaughtered.

AMANDA: But there may be something in there about setting a bad example to the nation's youth.

CAROLINE: The nation's youth don't watch me that much, do they?

LEO: Loads of people at college watch it.

CAROLINE: Do they?

LEO: Even supposedly intelligent people.

AMANDA: That particular audience demographic is certainly on the rise.

CAROLINE: It just makes me so angry.

AMANDA: And now for the bad news.

CAROLINE: I assumed *that* was the bad news?

AMANDA: *What* was the bad news, sorry?

CAROLINE: That I'm not setting a good example?

AMANDA: The bad news is that the commissioning editor may or may not want a meeting with you first thing in the morning.

CAROLINE: Lucinda wants a meeting?

AMANDA: Before you go live.

CAROLINE: Oh for God's sake!

AMANDA: I'll know more after I've spoken to Sarah.

AMANDA'S phone to her ear.

CAROLINE: It was a friend's birthday and yes I suppose we'd all had a little too much to…

AMANDA: Hi there, lovely. Sorry, you're breaking up.

CAROLINE: You have to go outside.

AMANDA: Hold on, darling, just extricating myself from Caroline's kitchen where we are it seems *sans reception.*

AMANDA goes outside again.

CAROLINE: People aren't really going to care about a photo of me being a little bit tipsy, are they?

LEO: Why did you just ask me about Ji-Woo?

CAROLINE continues with food prep etc.

Are you being serious?

CAROLINE: I have finally, after three decades of making them, I have finally, *finally* discovered how to make the perfect roast potato!

LEO: I'm delighted for you...

CAROLINE: The secret is *one* - only ever use Maris Piper potatoes; and *two* – once you've peeled them you always run them under cold water to drain all the starch.

LEO: Jesus, Mum...

CAROLINE: And *three* - before you cover them in hot oil you must first always cool them down in the fridge.

She removes peeled potatoes from the fridge.

LEO: Great.

CAROLINE: You see, it's actually the hot oil seeping into the cracks in the cooled potato that makes them so crispy.

LEO: I need to talk to you about...

CAROLINE: So if you could pour this into the roasting tray there, please.

LEO: *(Picking up a bottle of olive oil.)* This?

CAROLINE: And you like them with garlic and rosemary, yes?

LEO: I don't really care so...

CAROLINE: Ta-da!

She triumphantly produces the garlic and rosemary.

So if you could kindly press a whole bulb for me, my darling?

LEO: *(Doing so.)* Mum, could we please just…?

CAROLINE: Now listen, your father and I have been talking and we've decided we don't want you starting out in life owing the banks a small fortune.

LEO: But you *are* the banks.

CAROLINE: I see so we're supposed to keep on apologising for the fact he's spent his working life in the banking industry? Is that what you still want us to do? Does it really make us such evil people in your eyes?

LEO: Someone has to take responsibility.

CAROLINE: For what?

LEO: I don't know. For the state of the nation.

CAROLINE: Anyway what we'd really like to do, but only if you're happy about it, is to…

LEO: I need to tell you about my plans.

CAROLINE: …to completely write off your debts.

LEO: Say that again.

CAROLINE: Assuming you've been reasonably sensible.

LEO: Completely?

CAROLINE: That way you won't have all this appalling worry hanging over your head for the next few years.

A silence.

What do you think?

LEO: I don't know.

CAROLINE: Are you happy about that?

LEO: I wanted to pay my loans off myself.

CAROLINE: How?

LEO: And I have been earning anyway so…

CAROLINE: Have you?

LEO: Private Latin tuition.

CAROLINE: Your father is going to talk to you further about this but I wanted to give you the heads up.

LEO: The heads up?

CAROLINE: So how much do you owe?

LEO: About the average.

CAROLINE: How much is the average?

LEO: *(After a pause.)* Around fifty grand.

CAROLINE: Okay. Jolly good then. I'm not sure that's such a massive amount. In the great scheme of things.

LEO: But I sort of wanted to be self…

CAROLINE: Yes, I'm sure that will be perfectly acceptable.

A silence.

And what we also want to do is help you with buying your own flat.

LEO: Honestly, Mum…

CAROLINE: Well, what we're actually going to do is *buy* you your own flat.

LEO: All this is a bit…

CAROLINE: Anyway you mentioned something about your plans?

LEO: I did.

CAROLINE: So?

LEO: I'm going to Syria.

CAROLINE: I beg your pardon?

LEO: I'm volunteering to help the refugees in Syria.

AMANDA re-enters from outside.

AMANDA: Now it turns out Lucinda's not going to be here tomorrow morning but she *would* like a quick Skype conversation with you after we're done recording just so you can set her mind at rest about one or two things.

CAROLINE: What one or two things?

AMANDA: Well, one assumes about your various nocturnal activities.

CAROLINE: But I don't have any nocturnal…

AMANDA: *Excusez-moi.*

AMANDA exits to the hallway as CAROLINE continues.

LEO: I *was* going with Rory.

CAROLINE: Rory?

LEO: But now it seems I'm going alone.

CAROLINE: You're not serious about this, are you?

LEO: We have to actually *do* something!

CAROLINE: Your father will be absolutely furious.

LEO: We have to get out there and actually get our hands dirty.

CAROLINE: And that's of course commendable but…

LEO: And even though the climate's fucked beyond repair so...

CAROLINE: Of course it isn't!

LEO: And we'll probably all be dead by the end of the century.

CAROLINE: Of course we're not going to be ...

LEO: You not noticed how hot it is?

CAROLINE: It's the middle of June, Leo!

LEO: Mother Nature's burning us all away.

CAROLINE: It's just a lovely summer's day.

LEO: The revenge of Gaia.

CAROLINE: The revenge of who?

LEO: *Homo sapiens* is a deadly virus she's trying desperately to rid herself of.

CAROLINE: How can you be so negative?

LEO: Because my understanding of the world isn't channelled via the corporate media.

CAROLINE: What corporate media?

LEO: And I prefer to concern myself with the facts alone.

CAROLINE: But they are always *your* facts, Leo.

LEO: You're still a Bible reader, aren't you?

CAROLINE: Anyway you are *not* going to Syria!

LEO: And isn't there some story about Noah and the Flood?

CAROLINE: Do you hear me?

LEO: Where God drowns everyone for being so wicked?

CAROLINE: Do you?

LEO: And so stupid.

CAROLINE: Look, you've only just arrived, darling.

LEO: So the initial placement in Syria is two years.

CAROLINE: It gets so exhausting, all this.

LEO: And I'm starting in September.

CAROLINE: What exactly do you hope to do out there?

LEO: Perhaps a bit of teaching.

CAROLINE: Because you can't even drive.

LEO: But mainly manual labour.

CAROLINE: Manual labour? You?

AMANDA enters, followed by GRAEME.

AMANDA: ...and so if you wait there one second, my lovely, I shall forthwith text thee my number.

AMANDA locates her phone.

This lovely man here is going to be building me a new walk-in wardrobe.

GRAEME: Need to pick up the van, Caroline, so...

AMANDA: One assumes a detour down to Peckham to assist a young damsel in distress isn't going to tax thee overmuch?

GRAEME: Then I'll load up and be out your hair.

CAROLINE: You've done a fantastic job so...

AMANDA: It's south of the river.

GRAEME: I know where it is.

AMANDA: So when d'you think you could pop over?

GRAEME: I'll have to check.

AMANDA: I'm free all weekend now so...

LEO: I'm Leo by the way.

GRAEME: Graeme.

LEO: I'm her son.

GRAEME: Alright?

AMANDA: Could we not offer him a glass?

GRAEME/CAROLINE: I don't drink./He doesn't drink.

AMANDA goes to the kitchen area and locates wine glasses.

GRAEME: What's the champagne for?

CAROLINE: Leo's just graduated.

AMANDA: From Cambridge.

GRAEME: Course he has.

AMANDA/CAROLINE: With a First.

A silence.

AMANDA: *You* went to Cambridge, right?

CAROLINE: Oxford. I read Theology.

LEO: Which isn't even a real subject.

CAROLINE: Of course it's a real…

AMANDA: You get a First too?

CAROLINE: *(After a pause.)* No.

A silence.

AMANDA: Of course it was only the utter brutality of the real world for me.

CAROLINE: Yes, well, it isn't always necessary to…

AMANDA: When I was a girl in pigtails my mother was diagnosed with MS.

CAROLINE: Oh, that's the one where they find it rather hard to get out of bed?

AMANDA: That's ME.

CAROLINE: Of course it is. Yes. I knew that.

AMANDA: Multiple Sclerosis, Caroline, is a disease whereby the body's immune system, for some inexplicable reason, is directed against the body's central nervous system, causing in sufferers a gradual loss of mobility and cognitive powers. Not to mention of course bladder problems, bowel problems, sexual problems, visual problems, hearing problems, dizziness and extreme fatigue. All of which can be accompanied by an often debilitating depression.

A long silence.

But then your dear friend God does move in very mysterious ways, doesn't He?

CAROLINE: How do you mean exactly?

AMANDA: It couldn't be perchance that he actually *wants* us to suffer?

CAROLINE: I can quite understand why you're angry with God, Amanda, but…

AMANDA: Oh, I'm not even remotely angry with Him.

CAROLINE: I'm so happy to hear you say that because…

AMANDA: I just think he's a nasty old fuck.

A silence.

Anyway: my dad couldn't handle it. Being married to all that sickness and misery. Upped sticks and went to live in New Zealand with some trollop half his age. And was neither seen nor heard of ever again. And so single-handedly Yours Truly had to take care of my mother and

35

my two younger sisters and so yes that was me from the age of ten. Cooking, cleaning, working most weekends, wiping tears, wiping arses.

A silence.

CAROLINE: I empathise with your pain and your anguish, Amanda, but I believe what God actually intends is that...

AMANDA: There was very little punting down the jolly old river for me.

A silence.

CAROLINE: And so how's your mother now?

AMANDA: Died two and a half months ago.

CAROLINE: Really?

AMANDA: Well, I'm not making it up.

CAROLINE: Sorry, what I meant to say was...

AMANDA: I do *hope* she was dead when they lowered her into that hole in the ground.

CAROLINE: It's all so recent.

AMANDA: Anyhoo: praise be the Lord.

CAROLINE: You mustn't say things like that...

AMANDA: Day she died was the best day of my life.

A long silence.

LEO: So, Graeme, how long have you been a carpenter type person?

GRAEME: Not long.

CAROLINE: He used to be a professional footballer.

AMANDA: Now *that* is super sexy.

CAROLINE: But was forced to retire before he'd really got started.

LEO: Why?

GRAEME: Wrecked my cruciate ligament.

LEO: Who did you play for?

GRAEME: Luton Town.

LEO: Not that I know the first thing about football.

GRAEME: Made five appearance for the first team. Scored a goal in every game.

CAROLINE: The world was his oyster.

GRAEME: Then one mistimed tackle and my career's over.

AMANDA: Your dear little dream died right there and then in the grass?

GRAEME: You what?

LEO: So what did you do then?

GRAEME: I was shown the door basically. Spent a whole load of years cursing my fate, drinking too much and gradually losing all me mates. Then I hit my rock bottom, decided I still wanted to be part of this life and learned a new trade.

AMANDA: And so here you are?

GRAEME: So here I am.

CAROLINE: Well now, of course Jesus was a carpenter, wasn't he?

A long silence.

GRAEME: Anyway, mate. Really well done.

LEO: Thank you.

GRAEME: On passing your exams.

CAROLINE: A First no less.

A silence.

AMANDA: *(To GRAEME.)* So, my lovely, when you think I might be able to book you in? To come and give my bedroom a thorough inspection?

GRAEME: As I said, I'll have to see how I'm....

AMANDA: A good going over.

GRAEME: ...fixed.

AMANDA: Like I say, tonight I'm free or all day tomorrow...

GRAEME: Weekends are no good for me really so...

AMANDA: I'm sure I'll be able to keep him very, very busy.

CAROLINE: I may be able to find more work for him here actually.

GRAEME: In the house?

CAROLINE: In this area. I've a number of divorced friends who I know have work they...

AMANDA: That won't prevent him helping *me* out.

CAROLINE: Mind you, the ones who *do* have partners are always complaining about how useless they are in the DIY department.

AMANDA: Do we think there's currently a crisis of masculinity in this country?

CAROLINE: Where did all the real men go?

AMANDA: Indeed we diddly do.

CAROLINE: Who can fix things, who can actually *do* things?

AMANDA: All these funny little man boys mincing around with their ridiculous beards.

CAROLINE: Anyway it would save him having to traipse all the way down to Peckham or wherever else it is she lives.

AMANDA: *(To GRAEME.)* Where resideth thou?

GRAEME: You what?

CAROLINE: He lives in Totteridge and Whetstone.

AMANDA: In that case, he can easily…

CAROLINE: It'd be a real expedition for him to get over to you.

AMANDA: It's not that much of an expedition.

CAROLINE: We'll try to fix him up with something in North London.

AMANDA on her phone.

AMANDA: Yes, so what we can glean from our end is that these snaps are only going to be published online. Exactly, it's not as if she's been photographed shooting up or anything of that ilk. I have seen them, yes. Well, she mainly looks extremely wrecked, mascara running down her face in big, black, semi-tragic streams and she's sort of lying on her back on the pavement with her piggly-wiggly little legs flicking up in the air… Sorry, go on. You're breaking up.

CAROLINE: You have to go outside.

AMANDA: We have no reception down here so… Wait a moment, lovely.

AMANDA goes outside again.

GRAEME: What's all that about?

LEO: There's photos of Mum doing the rounds.

CAROLINE: Graeme's been doing some improvements to your bedroom for us.

LEO: Nice.

CAROLINE: Made me singlehandedly shift all his stuff from his much nicer room on the first floor all the way up to the top of the house.

GRAEME: It is a bit of a distance.

LEO: Wasn't quite singlehanded but…

CAROLINE: It nearly killed me.

LEO: Spent most of my time here barricaded away in my bedroom, earphones on, trying to block out the sounds of the two of them screaming at each other.

CAROLINE: That's not quite true but…

LEO: Or rather the sound of *him* screaming at *her*, with *her* endlessly saying sorry.

AMANDA re-enters from the garden.

AMANDA: It's all going to be absolutely tickety-boo.

CAROLINE: In what way?

AMANDA: Tickety-boo because people love you. Tickety-boo because they love your show. Tickety-boo because your book is selling like hot cakes so these photos aren't going to harm you. That is the considered view of the professionals.

CAROLINE: Really?

AMANDA sniffs very hard.

AMANDA: Oh, fuck me.

She wipes her nose with the back of her hand.

CAROLINE: Are you feeling alright?

AMANDA: I can honestly say that I have never, in all my twenty-five years upon this earth, felt better than I do this day.

AMANDA and CAROLINE drink.

LEO starts rolling a cigarette.

CAROLINE: What are you doing?

LEO: What does it look like I'm doing?

CAROLINE: It looks like you're rolling a cigarette?

LEO: That's because I am.

CAROLINE: Rolling a cigarette?

LEO: Rolling a cigarette, yes.

CAROLINE: Since when did you start rolling cigarettes?

LEO: About the same time I started smoking them.

CAROLINE: And when did you start smoking them?

LEO: About a year and a half ago.

CAROLINE: You know full well your father doesn't approve of cigarettes.

LEO: Then I'll smoke it outside.

CAROLINE: And neither do I.

LEO: Sorry about that.

CAROLINE: You do remember what cigarettes did to his mother?

LEO: I have been reminded once or twice, yes.

CAROLINE: But what you have to understand is that they are so terribly *bad* for you.

They all watch as she necks yet more wine.

LEO: Need to unpack my stuff so…

LEO leaves via the house.

CAROLINE: I cannot *believe* he's taken up smoking.

AMANDA: So, Graeme, will you be coming along to the BBC bash tomorrow night?

GRAEME: What bash is this?

AMANDA: *(On phone.)* Let me see if I can swing the man an invite.

CAROLINE: Why on earth would he want to go?

AMANDA: See how the other half live?

CAROLINE: What are you talking about?

AMANDA: See what the entitled metropolitan liberals of this land are doing with their days…

CAROLINE: I'm quite sure he would find it all utterly…

AMANDA: Cinderella, you *shall* go to the ball.

Phone to ear, AMANDA once again leaves for the garden.

(Exiting.) Hi there, lovely?

CAROLINE: It seems you have an admirer.

GRAEME: Well, she is pretty fit.

CAROLINE: If you like that kind of thing.

GRAEME: But clearly off her nut.

CAROLINE: I think she's just unhappy.

GRAEME: She can join the club then, can't she?

CAROLINE: Oh, Graeme, you're not so *terribly* unhappy, are you?

GRAEME: I much prefer the more mature woman myself.

A long silence.

CAROLINE: So…still no news about Greg?

GRAEME: Not yet.

CAROLINE: Still nothing from that school?

GRAEME: No-one's going to take him.

CAROLINE: You don't know that for certain, do you?

GRAEME: It's like having this big, angry dog in the house all the time.

CAROLINE: I can't imagine.

GRAEME: I love him to bits but…

CAROLINE: Of course you do.

GRAEME: But if life gives you lemons and all that bollocks…

A silence.

CAROLINE: You *could* let me help you?

GRAEME: No.

CAROLINE: I'd be happy to.

GRAEME: You've helped us enough.

CAROLINE: And if we could get you out of that pokey little flat then maybe things…?

GRAEME: I'll sort it myself.

CAROLINE: I could pay off some of your debts?

GRAEME: No! *(A pause.)* Thank you.

A silence.

Caroline, could you and me actually have a conversation?

CAROLINE: Now is not really a good time so…

GRAEME: I know…

A silence as she continues the food prep.

So then. Nothing more to be said then clearly.

CAROLINE: So… how much do we still owe you?

He hands her his invoice.

I have a small confession to make to you.

GRAEME: Oh, yeah?

CAROLINE: A terrible thought crossed my mind this morning. The kind of thought no Christian woman should ever entertain.

GRAEME: Go on.

CAROLINE: Oh, I shouldn't even be saying it out loud but…

GRAEME: Say it.

CAROLINE: I was lying awake and I could hear Mike snoring like a barnyard animal through the walls… Graeme, we are in separate bedrooms now and he still keeps me awake half the night with these atrocious noises of his.

GRAEME: Caroline, we've really got to work out what we're…

CAROLINE: And I found myself thinking… I found myself thinking if only… If only he would somehow… Somehow…

We hear the front door slam. They break apart.

GRAEME: I can't do this anymore.

Enter MIKE from the house, carrying his golf clubs. Leans the bag against the kitchen table.

MIKE: There was this chap, Caroline. Good ten, maybe fifteen, years younger than me. On the eighteenth hole. Fellow JP Morgan man I learned afterwards.

CAROLINE: Can I get you anything to…?

MIKE: And the four of us are packing up our clubs and watching the guys behind us and this chap, he's just played a pretty good shot onto the green and he's now walking over to his ball. Only about ten yards from the pin. And he's laughing his head off at something one of his mates has said, this massive smile on his face, wiping a tear away at one point and so he crouches down to eye up his shot and then, then he sort of goes all silent and he suddenly starts staring ahead, as if he's just seen a ghost or something. And then…bang…he keels over. Dies right then and there. Arse in the air, face on the grass.

CAROLINE: Oh, Mike, that's awful.

MIKE: Everyone's rushing around, very upset and making calls and the ambulance comes screeching onto the green and then his wife's there, I have to say, Graeme, for her age she was pretty decent crumpet actually. And she's there weeping and wailing and you know what I'm thinking?

CAROLINE: So he was only young then?

MIKE: I'm thinking "you lucky, lucky bastard."

CAROLINE: Because sixty is no age at all to…

MIKE: Out like a light doing something you love. With all your pals around you. In the open air and on a lovely summer's day. He's been spared the horrors of growing old, the horrors of slowly falling apart. No stroke, no cancer, no senile dementia for him.

CAROLINE: I'm not sure his wife would…

MIKE: On a brighter note however I did get my first ever hole in one.

CAROLINE: You finally got a…?

MIKE: Which is why I happen to be a tiny bit arseholed.

CAROLINE: Congratulations then.

MIKE: You a golfer, Graeme?

GRAEME: It's a bit of an expensive...

MIKE: I'm out there today and I'm thinking: all those lost hours, all those lost days, all those lost *years* of working, of meetings, in airless offices, in sterile conference rooms, when all that time I could have been out in the fresh air on some top-notch golf course. Because when you're utterly lost in a good game of golf, it takes your mind off the fact that you're over seventy, your whole body aches to buggery and you're having to get yourself ready for the Big Sleep...

CAROLINE: Please don't say depressing things like...

MIKE: And the reason the game of golf is so addictive, Graeme, is this: most of us hackers only hit two or three half-decent shots in a whole round so that when you do manage to hit that perfect shot, and I hit this magnificent, imperious drive off the thirteenth tee today, when you do manage to hit that shot, the endorphin rush is absolutely top notch. It's like everything in the entire universe comes together perfectly at that one particular moment.

CAROLINE: We were wondering, Mike, if you'd be able to write out a cheque for...?

MIKE: All goes still. All goes quiet. Your mind stops chattering. The swing is perfect, the sound your club makes through the air is perfect, the contact with the ball is perfect and it goes sailing up into the blue and Tiger Woods couldn't have hit it better and it bounces a couple of times on this beautiful, immaculate, velvety green and then slowly rolls towards the pin and then...kerplunk!... it drops out of sight and into the hole. And, oh, it's such a buzz. And your friends shake you by the hand or slap you on the back and you relish the applause, the applause which makes you feel all warm and tingly inside but then the next shot, the very next shot, off the very next tee, Graeme, is invariably a disaster and you're back to being a tired old amateur hacker once again.

AMANDA back in from the garden.

Now this delectable young creature is…?

CAROLINE: Amanda.

MIKE: Amanda, of course.

AMANDA: Nice to see you again.

MIKE: You're the one standing in for that rather surly, rather dusky maiden?

CAROLINE: The dusky maiden?

MIKE: Her with the… You know, the very… dusky maiden.

CAROLINE: You mean Prem?

MIKE: Even she.

CAROLINE: She was… *is* half-Indian.

MIKE: Whatever she was, she was very, very surly.

CAROLINE: She's having her baby so…

MIKE: Not to mention very, very dusky.

AMANDA: So how was your day hitting small white balls around large green fields with little metal sticks?

MIKE: Top notch, thank you.

AMANDA: Delighted to hear it.

MIKE: This one's got plenty of spunk in her.

AMANDA: Wouldn't go that far!

MIKE: Wouldn't you indeed?

AMANDA: *(To GRAEME.)* You'll be pleased to know, my lovely, you are now cordially invited to the end-of-series do tomorrow night.

GRAEME: I can't come so...

AMANDA: Oh, don't be such a spoilsport.

GRAEME: Got commitments.

AMANDA: Then can you not *un*commit yourself?

MIKE: Someone seems very keen for your company.

AMANDA: It's a night consuming fine wine and great food all at the expense of the unthinking licence fee payer.

GRAEME: I don't drink so...

CAROLINE: You'd absolutely hate it.

AMANDA: Please come, Graeme.

CAROLINE: Darling, terribly sorry, would you be able to write out this cheque for...?

AMANDA: Please.

MIKE: Which reminds me: did you speak to the boy?

CAROLINE: I did but I think he...

MIKE: And how did he receive the happy tidings?

CAROLINE: He was very...

MIKE: Paying off his student loans for him.

AMANDA: Lucky lad.

MIKE: Incidentally, Caroline, I spoke to Richard and he's looking at a two-bedroom flat for us, off the Caledonian Road somewhere, which because it's in need of extensive renovation is going for a bit of a song so I told him if we buy it for cash, we can do it up and then Leo can have it now as part of his inheritance.

CAROLINE: That'd be…

MIKE: Pointless keeping any spare capital in the high street, Graeme. Plough it all into property first chance you get.

GRAEME: Will do.

MIKE: Where *is* Leo by the way?

CAROLINE: He's upstairs at the…

MIKE: Then he needs to be *downstairs* so we can all start toasting his success.

CAROLINE: So, if you could write Graeme his cheque? You know, for the balance…

GRAEME passes MIKE his invoice, who inspects it.

MIKE: How about a thousand for cash?

GRAEME: If you like.

MIKE: Keep Tarquin the Tight-fisted Taxman out of proceedings?

MIKE screws up the invoice.

And pretend like none of this ever happened.

CAROLINE: Is that completely ethical, darling?

MIKE: *(To AMANDA.)* You wouldn't be a poppet and nip down to the cash machine for me?

AMANDA: You want *me* to go?

CAROLINE: I don't mind going so…

MIKE: I'm sure young Amanda here will be more than happy to oblige.

AMANDA: I'm not sure she's *that* happy to oblige.

MIKE: She is I believe paid to take care of my wife?

AMANDA: She is yes, but not by...

MIKE: So here's my PIN. And if you could withdraw a thousand for me then that would be top notch. You're an absolute angel.

AMANDA: I might run off with it.

MIKE: Then I shall have to hunt you down.

AMANDA battles with her anger. Then:

AMANDA: Remember, Caroline, you've got your Mrs Minto due shortly.

AMANDA leaves via the house.

MIKE: Who the hell is Mrs Minto?

CAROLINE: Our first viewing.

MIKE: *(A sudden rage.)* I'd really rather these things were taken care of when I'm not about. Last thing I want is complete strangers traipsing in and out of the house every evening.

CAROLINE: It's a necessary evil, is it not, when attempting to sell one's...

MIKE sits at the breakfast bar.

MIKE: I'm really, *really* feeling my age, you know.

GRAEME: I'll go then.

CAROLINE: Did you use any sunscreen today?

GRAEME: And be back in around...

CAROLINE: You look terribly red in the face.

MIKE: Where does all the time go?

CAROLINE: You need to stop worrying so much...

GRAEME, unheeded, leaves via the house.

MIKE: It's day after day after day after day...

CAROLINE: I know you don't like it when I talk about God but....

MIKE: Time's arrow is hurtling past and I can't keep track. All this time slipping so quickly through my fingers.

CAROLINE: The kingdom of heaven, darling, is here. It is here and it is now.

MIKE: I can feel my mind going. I can really feel it now, I keep forgetting things, I keep repeating myself and as for my bastard bladder...

CAROLINE: And as I keep telling you...

MIKE: I'm scuttling off to the bushes to piss every five minutes...

CAROLINE: ...you need to see Donald about your...

MIKE: I'm so frightened.

CAROLINE: I know you are.

MIKE: I feel the end coming.

CAROLINE: It's not remotely coming.

MIKE: All these voices in my head.

CAROLINE: You need to calm down.

MIKE: "You've wasted your life, Mike. You've thrown away all this precious time you've been given."

CAROLINE: And remember to focus on your breathing and...

MIKE: I've not been a very good person, have I?

CAROLINE: Oh, don't be so melodramatic...

MIKE: Not a very good father to the boy.

CAROLINE: It's okay.

MIKE: I don't know if he even…

CAROLINE: Not this again.

MIKE: …loves me.

CAROLINE: Of course he does.

MIKE: And if he does love me it's only in an unthinking biological way but he certainly doesn't *like* me.

CAROLINE: What is it, darling? Are you having one of your… one of your downturns?

MIKE: I'm so sorry about everything.

CAROLINE: It's alright.

MIKE: You're such a good person, such an *unbelievably* good person, and I'm perfectly aware of course that I am not. It's this depression. The black dog seems to come upon me more and more often…

CAROLINE: I know it does.

MIKE: I'm married to the most beautiful woman in the world. Who also happens to be the kindest and most forgiving woman in the world and so…

CAROLINE: We don't need to talk about this again.

MIKE: I really feel that this is the endgame for me.

CAROLINE: Why should it be the endgame?

MIKE: The Grim Reaper has one icy hand firmly upon my shoulder.

CAROLINE: This is so silly.

MIKE: I *know* I'm coming to the end of the road.

CAROLINE: Oh, Mike, please.

A silence.

MIKE: What time did you finally go to bed last night?

CAROLINE: Not long after you.

MIKE: And so you do… forgive me? For my little moment of madness?

CAROLINE: Come on, we're celebrating Leo's graduation.

MIKE: Tell me you forgive me?

A silence.

Caroline?

CAROLINE: I really don't know, Mike. It might take a bit of time for me to…

MIKE: All I want is for you to know the man I really am. And forgive me. Before I go. I want to know that at least one person in this world has known and loved me exactly as I am.

CAROLINE: You weren't ever actually in love with her, were you?

A silence.

Okay then… Let's just…

MIKE: It was all just a bit of an adrenalin rush, I suppose. A stupid ego trip. That some beautiful young creature like her could find an old fart lie me in any way attractive.

A silence.

And so have *you* ever…? You know? Oh, why am I even asking? I know you. I know how good you are, how loyal you are and how true. I know you don't have it in you.

CAROLINE: When I was a child and whenever I was called upon to make a wish, when I was blowing out candles on my birthday cake or pulling on a wishbone or whatever, you know what I'd always wish for? I'd wish that when

I was a grown up I'd meet someone and we'd love each
other so intensely, so passionately and so purely that the
thought of one of us dying and the other being left alone
in our old age would be simply unbearable. And so I'd
always wish that at the end of our lives my beloved and
I would be allowed to die together at exactly the same
moment and so...

MIKE: *(Exiting into the house.)* Now where *is* that exceedingly
clever son of mine? We're supposed to be celebrating the
capacity of his brain, are we not?

CAROLINE continues with the food prep. Drinks.

*After a time SALLY comes into the kitchen. Watches CAROLINE for
a time. Then:*

SALLY: Excuse me?

CAROLINE: Hello?

SALLY: Your friend. Amanda, is it? Just been chatting to her.
She said to come through.

CAROLINE: Oh, sorry, yes. I'm afraid I haven't had the
chance to get everything quite....

SALLY: I recognise the kitchen.

CAROLINE: ...ship-shape.

SALLY: From the TV.

CAROLINE: You like the show?

SALLY: Well, I've seen it.

CAROLINE: Anyway, do feel free to have a...

SALLY: Caroline Mortimer.

CAROLINE: Sorry?

SALLY: *The* Caroline Mortimer.

CAROLINE: Guilty as charged.

SALLY notices the champagne.

My son. He's just graduated. From Cambridge. History with a little Politics. Or Philosophy or…

SALLY: Congratulations.

CAROLINE: Leo's worked very hard and it hasn't always been easy and so, yes, we're all extremely…

SALLY: Leo the Lion, is it?

CAROLINE: I suppose it is.

A silence.

SALLY: *I'm* a Leo as it goes.

CAROLINE: Really?

SALLY: You call him that cos he was born under…?

CAROLINE: He's named after a sixteenth-century pope actually so…

SALLY: We're very loyal people. Us Leos.

A silence as SALLY continues, shyly, to look about.

CAROLINE: It's a super area for kids by the way. Do you live in London yourself?

SALLY: I love your fridge freezer.

CAROLINE: Do you have children?

SALLY: Two little boys.

CAROLINE: How lovely.

SALLY: Well, not so little now, of course.

CAROLINE: I see.

SALLY: Both like bloody giants all of a sudden.

CAROLINE: They do grow up fast, don't they?

SALLY: Too fast, if you ask me.

A silence.

CAROLINE: Well now, unfortunately, you have come at rather
an inconvenient time, for which I know you're not to
blame at all but if we could get on with this as quickly as…

SALLY: I'm not to blame at all.

CAROLINE: No. Of course.

A silence as SALLY examines the crucifix.

Anyway this is the kitchen. Obviously.

SALLY: Looks like he's in proper agony, doesn't it?

CAROLINE: He suffered for our sins.

SALLY: Nasty way to go.

CAROLINE: And so if you'd like to come this way then…?

SALLY: More of a Buddhist myself.

CAROLINE: I think all religions point to the same thing
essentially.

SALLY: What goes around comes around.

CAROLINE: Okay, well, if we could do this as quickly as we
can then…

SALLY: In the end we all get what's coming to us.

CAROLINE: I suppose we do.

SALLY: Cos, you see, I've never been a violent person.

CAROLINE: I'm sorry?

SALLY: Not really in my nature.

CAROLINE: I don't quite understand what you…

SALLY: But there's a big part of me that really wants to hurt you.

CAROLINE: Hurt me?

SALLY: You know, to pull out your hair, scratch out your eyes.

CAROLINE: I think you'd better leave.

SALLY: And I've been rehearsing this all day. What I'm going to say to you. What I'm going to do to your life.

CAROLINE: I'm sorry?

SALLY: Cos with you being famous and everything I was really, really nervous.

CAROLINE: I have absolutely no idea what you're...

SALLY: But now I'm actually here... With you stood here in front of me. Well, you're just an old woman, aren't you? I'll admit you look good for your age but, when it all boils down to it, you're not so much better than me.

CAROLINE: You're now starting to scare me.

SALLY: And I'm asking meself...why does he want you? You know, when he's got me? What have you got that I haven't? Why am I not enough for him?

CAROLINE: *(Penny dropping.)* Oh God, no...

SALLY: He left his phone at home this morning and I looked through his messages. And most of them are from you.

A silence.

CAROLINE: Is there any way we could have this discussion somewhere else?

SALLY: And some of them are utter filth, Caroline!

CAROLINE: Please.

SALLY: But what really got to me was this one from last night.

She takes out the phone.

"I love you, my darling Graeme. I love you with all my heart."

MIKE and LEO now into the kitchen, neither noticing SALLY.

MIKE: *(Raging.)* Did you give him permission to smoke cigarettes up there?

CAROLINE: Of course not!

MIKE: When he's the king of his own castle he can smoke himself to death if that's what he chooses…

CAROLINE: I'm sure he won't be doing it again so…

MIKE: Does he not remember what cigarettes did to his grandmother!?

CAROLINE: I did say, Leo, that your father…

MIKE: They had to cut half her windpipe out of her neck!

CAROLINE: …wouldn't be pleased.

MIKE: She had to speak through a fucking machine!

CAROLINE: Please, Mike, we have a…

MIKE: Spoke like a Dalek for the last two years of her life!

LEO: I am legally an adult so…

CAROLINE: It really is so silly, Leo.

MIKE: What's the point in getting a First at Cambridge if you're clearly so stupid you also choose to fill your lungs up with tars and poisons and various other…?!

SALLY: He could always try vaping.

A silence.

MIKE: Oh, sorry. Didn't see you there. Mike Mortimer.

SALLY: Nice to meet you.

MIKE: And this is my son. He's just graduated from Cambridge. My wife you've clearly already met.

SALLY: Bit star-struck actually.

CAROLINE: There's really…

MIKE: …no need to be.

CAROLINE: *(To SALLY.)* Could we go somewhere else to talk about this?

MIKE: Seems my house today is full to bursting with beautiful young creatures.

CAROLINE: We could maybe have a quick walk to the…?

MIKE: So why don't I give you a quick tour of the rest of my property?

SALLY: I only really came here to talk to your…

CAROLINE/MIKE: So if you'd like to come this way?

SALLY: I don't think you understand…

CAROLINE: Mike, I was actually trying to…!

With an arm around her waist he guides SALLY back out to the hallway.

LEO: Mum, I don't know who you are anymore.

CAROLINE: This isn't happening.

LEO: Who hell *is* "Caroline Mortimer" these days?

CAROLINE: Tell me this isn't happening.

LEO: Because I don't have the faintest idea.

CAROLINE: Please, please tell me that none of this is really happening.

A flash of lightning. A loud thunderclap.

[Note: if an interval is required it should take place here.]

59

LEO: Will you please look at me!?

CAROLINE: Oh God…

LEO: I want to know why you haven't told him yet.

CAROLINE: Will you excuse me, darling, just for a…

LEO: *(Grabbing her arm.)* Where are you going?

CAROLINE: I just need to speak to…

LEO: This is really important, Mum!

CAROLINE: Yes, but there's something happening right now
that…

LEO: This is really, *really* important!

She stops moving and grabs the kitchen top, breathing hard.

CAROLINE: Oh, Leo, I have done such a terrible thing.

LEO: Falling out of a taxi is hardly a terrible thing.

CAROLINE: You don't understand.

LEO: You gave me your word that by the time I'd graduated
you'd have…

CAROLINE: I know, I know…

LEO: And so if you don't tell him right now then I promise
you I'll…

CAROLINE: And, for God's sake, please don't mention this
silly idea of going off to…

LEO: In what way is it silly?

CAROLINE: Because it's yet another thing you've not thought
through properly.

LEO: You need to start putting me first for once!

CAROLINE: I *do* put you first.

LEO: You always put *him* first.

CAROLINE: He needs me.

LEO: *I* need you.

CAROLINE: Not as much as he does.

LEO: I've only had your voicemail for the last four months!

CAROLINE: I need a drink.

She drinks.

LEO: Don't you think you've had enough?

CAROLINE: Not remotely.

LEO: I've lost the love of my life.

CAROLINE: Yes, okay. Sorry. Tell me. Who has your heart been broken by?

LEO: Who do you *think* it's been broken by?

CAROLINE: I really don't know.

LEO: Yes, you do!

CAROLINE: So it wasn't by…Iwo-Jima?

LEO: What is the *matter* with you?

CAROLINE: I got her name wrong again, didn't I?

LEO: Why are you doing this to me?

CAROLINE: I'm not intentionally doing anything to you!

LEO: It's like you're completely insane.

CAROLINE: I'm sort of all over the place right now…

LEO: Is it because it goes against your stupid religion?

CAROLINE: My religion is not at all stupid!

LEO: I've had my heart broken by Rory! You understand? By Rory! Who is male!

CAROLINE: Can you please keep your voice down?

It now starts to rain outside. The rainfall increases throughout.

Rory is the...the Scottish chap?

LEO: *(Angry.)* Of course he's the Scottish chap!

A silence.

(Quieter.) Of course he's the Scottish chap.

CAROLINE: I really need to see what they're doing up there.

LEO blocks her exit.

LEO: I wanted to spend the rest of my life with him.

CAROLINE: *(Trying to get by.)* What are you doing?

LEO: Trying to talk to my mother!

CAROLINE: Okay, I know it's hard if you believe you love someone...

LEO: I don't just *believe* it!

CAROLINE: Alright then, I'm sorry!

LEO: It's a love that someone like you would *never* understand.

CAROLINE: I do know a little bit about these things.

LEO: If I wanted relationship advice then the last person in the world I'd come to would be you.

CAROLINE: Then why bring it up?

LEO: Because you're supposed to be my mother!

CAROLINE: I *am* your mother!

LEO: And I have to talk to someone!

CAROLINE: Would you excuse me, please?

LEO: I need your attention!

CAROLINE: It's just that your father isn't in a good place and...

LEO: It's always "your father, your father, your father."

CAROLINE: Relationships, long-term relationships, are difficult. Your father and I have been married for twenty-five years and so...

LEO: What does that even *mean*?

CAROLINE: It means a great deal.

LEO: Remaining married for any length of time is no accomplishment at all.

CAROLINE: Of course it is!

LEO: All it means is you've never had the courage to get yourselves divorced!

CAROLINE: Whatever you say, darling.

LEO: All I want... is for us to be close again.

CAROLINE: Oh and so do I, Leo...

LEO: But you've always worried more about him than you do about...

CAROLINE: He was completely unloved as a boy.

LEO: We know, we know...

CAROLINE: And so we just need to be kind.

LEO: But you don't have to let him dominate you!

CAROLINE: You know about his childhood. You know what your grandfather was like. Beat him up on a daily basis. His mother always took his father's side. Oh, come on, you know perfectly well what his parents were like!

LEO: I mean, what insanity, what vanity to knowingly bring children into this mess!

CAROLINE: Anyway, your father and I definitely need a change of scene now so…

LEO: But what about me?

CAROLINE: We're buying you this flat, aren't we?

LEO: You're both running off to Cornwall and I'm left…

CAROLINE: The time has come for me to be close to my mother. To try to salvage something from that relationship. I don't know how long she's going to last. But it could be decades.

LEO: But she's always been so cold to you.

CAROLINE: She's still my mother.

LEO: Cruel in fact.

CAROLINE: And I forgive her.

LEO: Has she asked for your forgiveness?

CAROLINE: Of course not. But she has it nonetheless.

A silence. From this point, due to the building storm, the lighting in the kitchen flashes on and off at various points.

Forgiveness is a gift we bestow upon ourselves, Leo. I forgive my mother for *my* sake, not for hers. In fact I'm sure she still believes she's always been a perfectly good parent. *(A pause.)* Your father's had a tough life, Leo. Way tougher than yours, way tougher than mine and so what he deserves is compassion.

LEO: I still don't see why you've stuck it out.

CAROLINE: Because I love the man.

LEO: Well, he's been no sort of father to me!

CAROLINE: The only thing I've ever wanted is for both of you to be happy.

LEO: Oh, for God's sake!

CAROLINE: Okay so you clearly don't know anything at all about real, grown-up love.

LEO: I know enough!

CAROLINE: What, you mean with that peculiar, mincing Scottish creature?

LEO: His name is Rory!

CAROLINE: For goodness sake, a little gay experiment at twenty-one is hardly enough to…

LEO: A little gay what!?!

CAROLINE: Now, if you'll excuse me, I really need to see what those two are doing so…

LEO: Don't worry, I'm leaving!

CAROLINE: Leaving!?

LEO: I'll stay at Adam's.

CAROLINE: No, no, please, darling! Please don't leave!

LEO: You're just not listening to me!

CAROLINE: I am listening, I am!

A silence.

Please, darling. Please talk to me.

LEO: From the outset we promised each other fidelity. Exclusivity. I demanded it. I demand it.

CAROLINE: I'm so sorry for saying 'experiment'.

LEO: Will you listen to me!?

CAROLINE: I'm sorry, I'm sorry…

LEO: But last night, last night when we're supposed to be out celebrating, I find out he's been...

CAROLINE: With other...?

LEO: With other...what?

CAROLINE: Well, people.

LEO: Massively. And behind my back.

CAROLINE: This is precisely why I've been so worried!

LEO: Care to explain?

CAROLINE: Because aren't all young men predominantly concerned with...?

LEO: What?

CAROLINE: Sex?

LEO: *You* tell *me*! You're clearly the expert!

CAROLINE: And without a woman to calm you down and temper your inclinations then...

LEO: Oh, the things you say.

CAROLINE: It seems that much harder to be happy?

LEO: And you breeders win all the prizes for that?

CAROLINE: I'm sorry then, I'm sorry!

A thunderclap (louder)

LEO: I asked him: isn't monogamy a small price to pay for the absolute honour of completely knowing and completely loving just one human being? For a whole lifetime?

A lightning flash.

He said that while he loves Italian food he doesn't see why he needs to eat it every single night of his life. Sometimes he might fancy an Indian or a Chinese or even...

CAROLINE: What on earth are those two doing up there?

LEO: ... a Doner kebab after closing time.

A silence.

I feel so hurt. So betrayed.

CAROLINE: We are all fallen souls in the eyes of God.

LEO: I'm sorry?

CAROLINE: Let those who are without sin...

LEO: Well, I'm here casting stones, aren't I?

CAROLINE: And you're wholly without sin, are you?

LEO: And so this rediscovery of your faith, is this why you've not told him yet?

CAROLINE: Because what we need to do is forgive.

LEO: Is it because of your stupid religion?

CAROLINE: Will you please stop calling it stupid?

LEO: It *is* stupid. It's probably the most stupid, intolerant thing there is in the world!

CAROLINE: *(A sudden rage.)* Maybe I haven't told your father yet because I've been hoping it's all an adolescent phase you'll eventually grow out of!!

MIKE and SALLY back into the kitchen.

MIKE: ...and when I say I'd like to be twenty-one again, I don't mean to myself at twenty one, to be Mike Mortimer at twenty one, because that would be like hell on earth, no I mean to be someone entirely different, someone who comes from a fully functional family, someone whose parents actually rejoiced in his existence...

LEO: *(To CAROLINE.)* Can't believe you actually said that.

SALLY: I'd love to live in a house this size.

MIKE: *(Offering SALLY to sit.)* To experience that time of life when one isn't simply a seething bundle of youthful anger and confusion.

CAROLINE: *(To MIKE.)* Is everything alright?

MIKE: Why shouldn't it be?

LEO: Can I have a word, Dad?

CAROLINE: *(To LEO.)* I just saw red, I'm sorry.

MIKE: And life's just flashed past me so quickly.

LEO: Could we go somewhere?

CAROLINE: Darling, please...

MIKE: One minute I'm young and full of beans and the next I'm a knackered old fucker who can barely get up in the mornings...

SALLY: You seem alright to me...

MIKE: Bless you, my darling, bless you...

CAROLINE: *(Taking LEO aside.)* This is neither the time nor the place to...

MIKE: But it does feel like my life's practically over before it's even started.

CAROLINE: Do you understand?

MIKE: *(Over to Leo.)* Just been saying, Leo, how wonderful it is to be twenty one, to be young, to be bright, to have the whole world at your feet.

CAROLINE: *(Over to SALLY.)* So you didn't say anything?

MIKE: Yes, lucky old Leo here will have his debts paid off for him and a flat of his own as he starts out on *his* journey.

CAROLINE: *(To MIKE.)* She didn't say anything?

MIKE: What are you talking about?

CAROLINE: *(To SALLY.)* Thank you.

MIKE: So we're expecting great things from the fruit of our loins here, aren't we?

CAROLINE: We are, yes, but…

SALLY: *(To CAROLINE.)* You think you can have everything, don't you?

MIKE: Who does, sorry?

LEO: Dad, I really need to tell you something.

SALLY: You've got everything anyway but still it isn't enough.

MIKE: Of course I had nothing at all when *I* started out.

CAROLINE: *(To SALLY.)* Perhaps you and I could go through to the other room?

MIKE: *My* father never dished out so much as a penny to me.

SALLY: If you like.

MIKE: Dished out plenty of beatings but rarely much cash.

CAROLINE: I'm just taking our guest through to the…

MIKE: Poor as church mice we always were.

LEO: Dad?

MIKE: He was a Japanese POW. Survived the Death Railway. You know, Bridge over the River Kwai and all that.

CAROLINE: *(To SALLY.)* So if you'd care to come this way…

MIKE: Don't drag her away, darling, because she's about to help us drink this bubbly.

LEO: Dad?

CAROLINE: Not now, Leo, please…

MIKE: Monsters the Japanese. Took pleasure in torturing, beheading, beating men to death.

SALLY: My brother was in the army actually.

MIKE: Yes, this lovely lady here tells me her brother proudly served his country in Afghanistan.

SALLY: My twin brother.

MIKE: Twenty-one years of age, Leo.

A silence.

CAROLINE: Is he okay?

SALLY: Killed himself a week after coming home.

MIKE uncorks the champagne with a loud pop.

A long silence.

CAROLINE: I am so, so sorry.

MIKE: Yes, of course. As am I. I really didn't realise.

MIKE pours the champagne.

CAROLINE: I honestly don't think that...

SALLY: When he died I totally lost it. Spent a week on a ward with a load of other broken folk. They sectioned me. That's what they call it. When you're detained under the Mental Health Act against your will.

MIKE passes SALLY a flute.

They tell me I shouldn't drink but...

MIKE: I'm sure one won't hurt, will it?

SALLY: I suppose not.

A silence.

MIKE: Well, anyway, good health, everyone.

LEO: To better times.

SALLY: To better times.

MIKE and SALLY touch glasses.

MIKE: Caroline?

CAROLINE: To better times, yes.

SALLY: To much better times.

A silence as they drink.

MIKE: Unfortunately the odd war does seem to be a necessary evil on this crazy old planet of ours.

SALLY: Goes to straight to your head, doesn't it?

MIKE: My father was a profoundly decent chap *before* the fall of Singapore apparently. Though sadly I only knew him afterwards, of course. When he wasn't.

LEO: Can I have a word now, Dad?

MIKE: I was born a few years after the War, you understand. But people do tell me I look far younger than my years.

SALLY: Do they?

MIKE: *(To CAROLINE.)* Don't they?

CAROLINE: They do but…

MIKE: Do *you* think I look younger than my years?

SALLY: I think you look…

MIKE: How I loathe and detest growing old.

He pours SALLY more champagne.

SALLY: Ta.

MIKE: I've had problems with my teeth, my ears, my eyes, my back, my hands, my knees, my chest and even with my anal sphincter muscle, would you believe.

CAROLINE: Mike…

MIKE: *Anno Domini* is an absolute pain in the posterior.

LEO: At least you've had the opportunity.

MIKE: I'm sorry?

LEO: Of growing old.

CAROLINE: *(To SALLY.)* Perhaps I could show you the rest of the house?

MIKE: That's quite correct of course.

LEO: Unlike this lady's poor brother.

A silence.

MIKE: Put me in my place there, hasn't he?

CAROLINE: So shall we go?

MIKE: Put me firmly in my place.

SALLY: Can't remember the last time I had champagne.

MIKE: *(Filling SALLY's glass.)* You have to reserve it for the special occasions, don't you?

SALLY: I've had too much already.

CAROLINE: *(To SALLY.)* Would you care to follow me?

MIKE: What is it you said your other half does again?

SALLY: I didn't.

MIKE: Is he in finance or law or advertising or…?

SALLY knocks her glass back in one.

Steady as she goes.

CAROLINE: So the garden is just through here and..?

SALLY: I shouldn't have done that really.

CAROLINE: It's just this way then…

CAROLINE guides SALLY towards the garden exit.

MIKE: *(His arm around her.)* If I might make so bold, your husband is one hell of a lucky guy.

SALLY: Don't think *he* thinks so.

MIKE: Well, he should think so.

SALLY: I'll tell him when I see him.

MIKE: You tell him from me.

SALLY: I will.

MIKE: You tell him from me.

CAROLINE: Mike, I'm just trying to…?

SALLY: Feeling a bit sloshed already.

MIKE: As am I.

SALLY: I don't really drink as a rule.

MIKE: It's the only way to be.

SALLY: Is it?

MIKE: Isn't that right, darling?

CAROLINE: I'm sorry?

MIKE: A little bit sloshed.

CAROLINE: What about it?

MIKE: It's the only way to be.

CAROLINE: I don't know about that.

MIKE: We like getting a bit sloshed in this house.

SALLY: Do you?

MIKE: Especially my wife here.

CAROLINE: Mike, please…

MIKE: She *loves* getting a bit sloshed.

SALLY: Does she?

MIKE: Don't you?

CAROLINE: Mike, please....

MIKE: It's why I play so much golf actually. It's because I never know which Caroline Mortimer I'm going to be coming home to.

CAROLINE: We're just going through to the garden.

MIKE: The sloshed Caroline Mortimer.

CAROLINE: *(To SALLY.)* Okay so if you'd...?

MIKE: Or the not-so-sloshed Caroline Mortimer. Which are you at the moment, darling? Are you the sloshed Caroline Mortimer or are you the not-so-sloshed Caroline Mortimer?

CAROLINE: I am the... the not-sho-shloshed Caroline Mortimer.

MIKE: *(Laughing.)* She says she's the not "sho shloshed" one.

His arm still around SALLY, he laughs alone at his own wit.

I envy you, you know. Being so young and so beautiful and starting out upon your life.

CAROLINE: Yes, but could you let go of her now?

MIKE: Man at the club today, far younger than me. Just like that: keeled over and croaked. Face on the grass, arse in the air. *(A pause.)* Lucky bastard.

LEO: I've got something to say, Dad.

MIKE: Perhaps we should wait until after I've shown our potential buyer the rest of the...

LEO: But I want to tell you *now*.

CAROLINE: Please, Leo...

MIKE: *(To SALLY.)* You have to see our new gazebo.

CAROLINE: So how was your golf today?

MIKE: I already said?

CAROLINE: And you all had a lovely day?

MIKE: Top notch.

CAROLINE: That's good.

MIKE: I already said.

CAROLINE: *(To SALLY.)* So let me show you outside then...

MIKE: But *I* want to show her!

CAROLINE: I'm going to show her, Mike!

MIKE: It's not every day I get to spend time with such a beautiful young woman.

SALLY: Your wife is a beautiful woman.

MIKE: But sadly not so young anymore!

MIKE laughs uproariously but no-one else does. The laugh peters out.

Nobody speaks.

Outside the rain is falling more heavily, the light outside darkening.

LEO: Dad?

MIKE: So, yes. This important thing then?

LEO: I want you to know that...

CAROLINE: ...he's very happy about the money.

MIKE: What money?

CAROLINE: Us paying off his student loans.

MIKE: Yes, you already said.

CAROLINE: Of course I did.

MIKE: *(Laughing.)* Hope you're not getting early-onset Alzheimer's over there!

SALLY: *(To CAROLINE.)* See, if you're gonna take something away from me that I love…

MIKE: What did she say?

SALLY: Then *I'm* gonna take something away from you that *you* …

CAROLINE: Mike, are you going to take a shower before we eat?

MIKE: Of course I am, of course I am…

CAROLINE: Well, why don't you go now then?

MIKE: Surely it would be rude to this lady who's come here to…

SALLY: Don't worry about me.

MIKE: *(To LEO.)* And so you're happy about us buying the flat?

LEO: I suppose so.

MIKE: You suppose so?

CAROLINE: Of course he's happy!

MIKE: He "supposes" so, Caroline?

LEO: But first I've something of a bombshell to drop.

MIKE: Think of it as having some of your inheritance early.

SALLY: Can I use your toilet?

MIKE: What kind of a bombshell?

CAROLINE: *(To SALLY.)* I'll come with you and then…

SALLY: I think I'm gonna be sick.

MIKE: What's he mean, a bombshell?

CAROLINE: There's a toilet through there.

SALLY: Thank you.

CAROLINE: I'll show you.

The women move over to exit towards the house.

SALLY exits but MIKE holds CAROLINE by the arm.

MIKE: What's he mean, a bombshell?

CAROLINE: Could you let go of my arm, please?

LEO: Shall we go to the pub, Dad?

MIKE: What for?

CAROLINE: But supper's almost ready!

LEO: For a drink.

MIKE: We never go to the pub?

LEO: I know but...

MIKE: For a drink or for anything else.

CAROLINE: Mike, I'm just showing our viewer out.

MIKE: But I've only shown her half the house!

LEO: First time for everything.

MIKE: So what do you think about the idea?

LEO: Which idea?

MIKE: The buying you a flat idea?

LEO: Will you *please* listen to me?

CAROLINE: Not now, Leo, please!

MIKE: We reckon we should be able to sort you out with a
    two-bed somewhere so you could maybe let out the other
    room to a friend. Have a little income stream going on.

While of course at the same time it'd mean you wouldn't be completely on your own.

CAROLINE: So why don't you have your shower and then we can start enjoying our evening?

MIKE: We will after I've shown Mrs Minto the…

CAROLINE: Mike, that woman is not remotely interested in buying the house, okay!

MIKE: Of course she is!

CAROLINE: She's just a timewaster.

MIKE: Now your mother does worry about you being lonely…

CAROLINE: She's just a fan of the show!

MIKE: …but I said to her Leo's not the sort of chap to be afraid of his own company so…

LEO: How would *you* know?

MIKE: Sorry?

LEO: How would you know what 'sort of chap' I am?

MIKE: I feel I *do* know you reasonably well.

CAROLINE: Leo, don't do this now!

LEO: You know me so well you don't even know what sexuality I am.

MIKE: What?

CAROLINE is about to exit.

LEO: You didn't know I was gay, did you?

She stops in her tracks.

MIKE: Gay?

LEO: Gay.

MIKE: What do you mean, gay?

LEO: What do you mean, what do I mean?

MIKE: I mean, what do you mean?

LEO: I mean that I'm gay.

CAROLINE: Leo, please…

MIKE: You are of course joking?

LEO: Am I?

MIKE: Aren't you?

LEO: You'd better ask *her.*

MIKE: Is he winding me up?

CAROLINE: Oh God…

MIKE: He can't really be gay, can he?

LEO: He is.

MIKE: Is he?

CAROLINE: So he says.

LEO: I'm sorry?

MIKE: He's telling me he's gay?

LEO: That's because I am.

CAROLINE: I was hoping this was a conversation we could
have at another…

MIKE: What about Iwo-Jima?

CAROLINE: Ji-Moo.

LEO: Ji-*Woo.*

CAROLINE: That's what I meant.

MIKE: And what about all these other birds?

LEO: What other birds?

MIKE: *(To CAROLINE.)* He's been playing the field, you said?

CAROLINE: Mike…

LEO: Playing the field?

MIKE: But not met anyone he wants to bring home yet?

LEO: You told him I was playing the field?

CAROLINE: All I said was that…

LEO: You need, Dad, to know that I'm gay. That I've always been gay. That I always will be gay. And that I am not, despite what my mother thinks, ever going to grow out of it.

CAROLINE: I didn't mean it like that…

MIKE: So this is really true?

CAROLINE: I'm afraid so.

LEO: You're *afraid* so?

CAROLINE: I didn't mean it like that…

LEO: How *did* you mean it then?

MIKE: *(To CAROLINE.)* How long have you known?

CAROLINE: I think we all need to…

MIKE: *(To CAROLINE.)* How long have you known this?

LEO: She's known for years.

MIKE: For *years*?

LEO: At least since the sixth form.

CAROLINE: I have *not* known since the sixth form!

MIKE: So you've been lying to me?

CAROLINE: Sort of.

MIKE: Sort of?

CAROLINE: I suppose.

MIKE: You suppose?

LEO: Sort of, you suppose?

MIKE: Why would you lie to me?

CAROLINE: Because…

MIKE: Why would you lie to me about a thing like this?

CAROLINE: …I didn't think you'd be all that happy about it.

MIKE: I am *not* all that happy about it!

Unseen SALLY re-enters the kitchen.

LEO: Dad?

MIKE: I just don't understand.

LEO: You don't understand what?

MIKE: You were always such a keen rugby player.

MIKE now slowly exits to the garden.

CAROLINE: I so wish you hadn't done that.

LEO: It's pissing down out there.

CAROLINE: I so, *so* wish you hadn't done that.

LEO: I told you I would.

CAROLINE: He's mentally very fragile at the moment.

LEO: You promised me you'd tell him.

CAROLINE: As am I.

LEO: You gave me your absolute word.

CAROLINE: And we also have this crazy woman in the house.

LEO: I'm shaking actually.

SALLY: That's not very nice.

A silence.

CAROLINE: I'm sorry, I didn't see you there.

SALLY: Takes all sorts to make a world, you know.

LEO: You should have told him.

CAROLINE: I didn't mean 'crazy'.

MIKE: *(Off, loud.)* Jesus H Christ!

A silence in the kitchen.

LEO: Bang goes my inheritance then.

MIKE: *(Even louder.)* Jesus H Chriiiist!

MIKE, soaked, now returns. He grabs a bottle of scotch from a cupboard. Takes a glass. Sits. Pours. Drains the glass.

CAROLINE: Everything alright?

MIKE: Of course. Why wouldn't it be?

CAROLINE: I see.

MIKE: So: my son and heir is a homosexual. That's perfectly fine. That's perfectly good.

LEO: What you've sometimes termed a bender. An uphill gardener. A sausage jockey.

CAROLINE: Oh, he's never called them that!

LEO: What d'you mean "them"?

CAROLINE: And if he did he only ever meant it in jest…

LEO: And I've never *ever* played the field.

MIKE: Well, I apologise if I ever really did say those things.

A silence.

My son is a homosexual Bolshevik vegetarian!

LEO: I'm a vegan.

MIKE: Leo, would you please define the word VEGETARIAN?

LEO: Sorry?

MIKE: Vegetarian is Neolithic for…wait for it, wait for it… ABSOLUTELY SHIT AT HUNTING.

MIKE now laughs wildly. The laughter builds and soon becomes uncontrollable as the others watch in awkward silence. Eventually he calms down, wiping away his tears.

Heard that at the golf club. It's absolutely priceless.

CAROLINE: *(To SALLY.)* So sorry about all this.

SALLY: So you think I'm crazy, do you?

CAROLINE: Not at all.

SALLY: Cos I *can* show you crazy, if you want?

MIKE: What's going on?

CAROLINE: I'm showing this lady out.

MIKE: But I haven't yet shown her the attic room.

CAROLINE: Sorry?

MIKE: I haven't yet shown her Leo's room.

LEO: *I* can show her.

CAROLINE: Because supper's as good as ready.

SALLY: I got something to tell you as well.

MIKE: You have?

SALLY: I got me own little announcement to make…

MIKE: What kind of announcement?

A silence.

SALLY: I just wanted to say…

A silence.

I just wanted to say…

MIKE: Yes?

CAROLINE: Oh God…

SALLY: *(Picking up a framed photo.)* Who's the baby?

LEO: That's me, I believe.

SALLY: What a gorgeous little thing, Caroline.

LEO: I remember such happy days being sat just here in my highchair.

MIKE: It's a scientifically accepted fact that we have no real memories before the age of three.

SALLY: Well, I remember being in my mother's womb.

MIKE: You may *think* you do but I'm afraid…

SALLY: What's more: I also remember every single one of my past lives.

LEO escorts SALLY towards the hallway.

CAROLINE: Where are you going?

LEO: I'm showing her my room.

CAROLINE: But I don't really want you two…

SALLY: Don't worry, Caroline. I'll be very, very gentle with him.

CAROLINE: No, seriously…

They leave the kitchen.

MIKE: What's the *matter* with you tonight?

CAROLINE: Then I'll come with you!

MIKE: *(Pulling her back into the kitchen.)* Seriously, what kind of marriage do we have, what kind of marriage do we have if you keep a thing like this a secret from me? For all these years.

CAROLINE: Mike, will you kindly stop manhandling me!

MIKE: Why would you lie? Telling me about all these girlfriends he's never had, telling me he's not met anyone he's serious enough about, telling me he's just been waiting for the right woman...

CAROLINE: I was trying to protect you. I've been very worried about your mental...

MIKE: You lied and you lied and you lied!

CAROLINE: But that woman now upstairs with our son seems to be completely...

MIKE: He was trembling just then. Trembling like a child. He was scared of how I'd react. Am I really such an unapproachable father?

CAROLINE: He loves you, Mike...

MIKE: I so need us to be close again.

CAROLINE: But you really need to tell him.

MIKE: Tell him what?

CAROLINE: That you love him.

MIKE: I *do* love him.

CAROLINE: Then you need to tell him.

MIKE: I *have* told him.

CAROLINE: You have *never* told him.

MIKE: That's not true.

CAROLINE: You have never said the actual words.

MIKE: Again, untrue.

CAROLINE: He says he's never heard you say it.

MIKE: But he knows it.

CAROLINE: No, he doesn't.

MIKE: Of course he does.

CAROLINE: Mike, he needs your love. Your approval. You need to tell him how proud you are of him.

MIKE: I *am* proud of him.

CAROLINE: You need to put an arm around him.. You know, I've never seen you hug him once in his entire life.

MIKE: I *am* proud.

CAROLINE: And he says he can't remember you ever showing *me* any love.

MIKE: Showing *you*?

CAROLINE: No public displays of affection.

MIKE: Rubbish.

CAROLINE: No kissing, no touching. No tender words.

A silence.

MIKE: But I *do* love you.

CAROLINE: I know you do but...

MIKE: I just wasn't brought up to be especially...

CAROLINE: I know, I know....

MIKE: Tell me you're not going to leave me.

CAROLINE: Of course not.

MIKE: Because of my stupid little mistake?

CAROLINE: Mike, you're my husband...

MIKE: Because the thought of being an old man and slowly falling to pieces all on my own...

CAROLINE: It's alright.

She holds him in his distress.

MIKE: So you do forgive me? You can actually say that you do...?

CAROLINE: Mike, please.

MIKE: I don't want to be alone, Caroline. I really don't want to die alone!

AMANDA re-enters from the hallway, soaking wet, wired.

AMANDA: Love's young dream, eh?

MIKE: I beg your pardon?

AMANDA: So it seems Lucinda was at Cambridge with the features editor and they are still rather good chums.

She hands MIKE a fistful of new banknotes.

(To CAROLINE.) So, my lovely, they're more than happy to refrain from publishing the offending photographs...

MIKE: What offending photographs?

AMANDA: ...provided you are prepared to furnish them with a warts-and-all interview.

MIKE: What offending photographs?

AMANDA: Where you talk about your depression and your drinking problem...

CAROLINE: But I'm not sure I have a problem, have I?

AMANDA: Get your defence in first kind of thing.

MIKE: What defence?

CAROLINE: My defence?

MIKE: Who says she has a drinking problem?

AMANDA: So I said you'd agree.

CAROLINE: Mike, will you let go of me, please?

AMANDA: Methinks it's the least worst option.

CAROLINE: When would I have to do it?

AMANDA: Tomorrow after the show.

MIKE: And what depression?

AMANDA: Graeme's on his way in as well...

CAROLINE: Oh God, no...

AMANDA: Do we know if he's married at all?

MIKE: I believe he is.

AMANDA: Happily or unhappily, do we know?

MIKE: He has two sons.

AMANDA: Happily married or unhappily married, tis nae matter.

MIKE: Why does she speak like this?

AMANDA: Like what, sorry?

MIKE: Like you're on something?

CAROLINE: Mike, please...

MIKE: *Is* she on something?

AMANDA: *(Pouring.)* Any bubbly wubbly going spare?

MIKE: *(To CAROLINE.)* And what's this about you being depressed?

CAROLINE: Please, Mike, I just need to...

MIKE: *(Releasing her.) I'm* the one who's depressed!

CAROLINE is about to exit just as GRAEME enters.

GRAEME: Alright?

MIKE: *(To GRAEME.)* I'm the one's who's bi-bloody-polar!

AMANDA: We were just talking about you.

CAROLINE: *(Holding his arm.)* Graeme, could I have a quick word?

GRAEME: What about?

CAROLINE: Just about maybe doing an extra little job?

MIKE: What extra little job?

AMANDA: Wondering whether or not you were happily married.

GRAEME: Why you wanna know?

CAROLINE: If you could follow me?

AMANDA: *(Mimicking his accent.)* Why you *think* I wanna know?

GRAEME: I don't talk like that, do I?

AMANDA: Because nobody's really *happily* married, are they?

GRAEME: Aren't they?

CAROLINE: Graeme?

AMANDA: *(To MIKE.)* Are they?

MIKE: You asking *me*?

AMANDA: I'm asking *you.*

MIKE: I'm *very* happily married.

AMANDA: Well, *she* isn't!

MIKE: You referring to my wife?

AMANDA: Are you?

We hear glass smash outside as the wind approaches gale force.

GRAEME: It's crazy out there. Trees in the road, roof tiles flying about, people being lifted off their feet.

MIKE: Won't you stay for a quick drink?

CAROLINE/GRAEME: He doesn't drink./I don't drink.

AMANDA: What you doing tonight?

GRAEME: Going home.

CAROLINE: He has a family, Amanda.

GRAEME: Unfortunately.

AMANDA: You need to learn to live a little.

GRAEME: *(Hands MIKE a key.)* One front door key.

A silence as GRAEME waits for his cash.

Anyway, I really have to get home now so…

MIKE: Did we show our prospective buyer the garden by the way?

CAROLINE: Mike, if you could give Graeme his money now, please ?

MIKE: Doesn't seem like the kind of woman to have several million tucked up her sleeve.

CAROLINE: Because he needs to get off home.

GRAEME: What about this extra little job?

AMANDA: By the way I forgot to mention: Mrs Minto is running extremely late. Estate agent called while I was at the bank.

MIKE: What do you mean, running late?

AMANDA: Stuck she is in traffic.

MIKE: Why does she talk like this?

CAROLINE: Graeme is waiting for his money, Mike!

AMANDA: Due methinks to the inclement weather.

MIKE: So who is that woman currently upstairs with my son?

AMANDA: No idea.

CAROLINE: Oh, for God's sake…

CAROLINE takes the cash from MIKE's hand and passes it to GRAEME who puts it in his shirt pocket.

MIKE: *(To CAROLINE.)* What are you doing?

AMANDA: But Mrs Minto she most certainly is not.

MIKE: If she's not here to buy our house then who the hell is she?

AMANDA: So there's nothing at all I can do to persuade you?

GRAEME: You what?

AMANDA: To buy a young girl a drink tonight?

GRAEME: I can't, sorry.

AMANDA: What about this BBC bash tomorrow?

CAROLINE: For crying out loud, Amanda! Can you not see that Graeme is not remotely interested in you so why can't you just leave the poor bloody man alone?

A silence.

AMANDA: An interesting little outburst, if I might make so bold.

CAROLINE: Don't you think having an affair with one married man is enough for you?

AMANDA: Are you wanting a fight with me, Caroline?

CAROLINE: Of course I'm not wanting a fight!

AMANDA: Because don't think I haven't noticed the way you stare all longingly at him.

MIKE: What does she mean, longingly?

CAROLINE: Graeme, I think you'd better leave…

MIKE: I think you'd better leave, young lady.

AMANDA: "I think you'd better leave, young lady."

MIKE: I no longer want you on my premises.

Not without some force, MIKE ushers AMANDA out towards the front door.

AMANDA: *(In tears.)* Tell you what, Caroline. You can fuck your job! And all your pretend friends! And your pretend family and all your desperate, no-talent pretend celebrities. And you can fuck your aromatic plums and your marinated quails. And your Normandy pork and your artisan bread. And you can fuck your duck salads delicately drizzled with acacia honey. And your peach pies and your tiramisus and every single one of your macerated fucking strawberries!

MIKE has now forced her out of the kitchen.

MIKE: *(Off.)* We are your elders and we are your betters and we will *not* be spoken to in this way!

AMANDA: *(Back on.)* And you can fuck the two million fuckwits who watch you every week and who never for a single second suspect the whole thing's just a charade and a sham and one big, stupid, slop bucket of cynical, self-satisfied, middle-class bullshit!

She is dragged off. We hear the front door slam off.

CAROLINE: Your wife's here!

GRAEME: What?

CAROLINE: She's upstairs with Leo!

GRAEME: Don't fuck about, Caroline!

CAROLINE: You told me she never left the house!

GRAEME: She doesn't!

CAROLINE: Well, she's here now and she knows about us!

GRAEME: She can't do!

CAROLINE: You need to get her out of here.

GRAEME: Of course!

CAROLINE: You left your phone at home this morning.

GRAEME: I know I did.

CAROLINE: And she's been through your messages.

GRAEME: Ah shit!

CAROLINE: Why didn't you just delete my messages!?

GRAEME: I thought I had!

CAROLINE: All you had to do was delete my messages, Graeme!

Now MIKE re-enters.

MIKE: She's still out on the pavement, screaming abuse.

CAROLINE: Oh God…

MIKE: Whose idea was it to employ her?

CAROLINE: Not mine.

MIKE: Because that dusky girl was surly…

CAROLINE: Her name is Prem.

MIKE: But give me surly over stark, staring mad any day.

CAROLINE: What she wants is love.

MIKE: What she wants is locking up.

CAROLINE: She's had a hard life.

MIKE: We've *all* had a hard life!

Now LEO on from the hallway.

LEO: Everything alright down here?

MIKE: It is now.

LEO: Heard a commotion.

MIKE: Been ejecting an unwelcome visitor.

CAROLINE: Are you alright, darling ?

LEO: Why shouldn't I be?

CAROLINE: She didn't say anything then?

LEO: Like what?

MIKE: Where *is* that woman?

LEO: Being sick.

CAROLINE: Being sick?

LEO: In the upstairs lavatory.

MIKE: Because she is not who she says she is.

LEO: Who does she say she is?

MIKE: She says she's Mrs Minto.

LEO: Who's Mrs Minto?

MIKE: Who she says she is.

LEO: But she isn't Mrs Minto?

MIKE: Mrs Minto is the woman meant to be looking at the house.

LEO: And that's not her?

MIKE: She is not Mrs Minto.

LEO: I feel now like a great weight's been lifted off my shoulders.

MIKE: Look, what I want to say is… I am extremely… We are both extremely… Your mother and I are both extremely…

LEO: Extremely?

CAROLINE: What do we do, Graeme?

MIKE: What I mean is your revelation tonight isn't something which…

LEO: *(To GRAEME.)* I happen to be gay.

GRAEME: We know.

MIKE: *(To GRAEME.)* What did you say?

LEO: And I'm finally out.

MIKE: *You* knew about this?

GRAEME: What I mean is…

MIKE: *(To CAROLINE.)* You told Graeme before you told me?

CAROLINE: Of course not!

LEO: And I suddenly feel in a celebratory mood.

MIKE: Why did you tell *him* before you told *me*?

LEO: So I think I *will* have a drink.

LEO pours himself a glass as SALLY enters from the hallway.

MIKE: Would you kindly tell us who you are?

SALLY: Who I am?

MIKE: We would like to know why you are not Mrs Minto?

SALLY: Who?

MIKE: We understood you were a Mrs Minto?

SALLY: Don't know who that is.

MIKE: And you are clearly not she?

SALLY: Don't think so.

MIKE: We understood you were here to view the property?

SALLY: Don't think so.

LEO: Top-up for you, Mother?

CAROLINE: No, thanks.

LEO: For you, Madame?

LEO pours SALLY a glass.

MIKE: So perhaps then you would care to introduce yourself?

SALLY: Name's Sally. Sally Mackie.

She knocks back her glass in one.

MIKE: Mackie?

LEO: I should like to propose a toast.

MIKE: Why am I familiar with that name?

SALLY: Any more where that came from?

MIKE: Seen that name written down recently.

LEO fills her up.

(To GRAEME.) Yes, *you're* a Mackie, are you not?

LEO: To Leo Mortimer.

MIKE: *(To SALLY.)* This is Graeme. He's been doing some
work for us.

SALLY: I know who he is.

MIKE: How so?

96

SALLY: He's my husband.

CAROLINE: Oh God...

LEO: On the event of his graduation.

MIKE: Oh, so this is your wife then?

LEO: And also of course...

MIKE: So why have we been showing you around my house?

SALLY: Thought you were just being friendly.

LEO: ...on the first day of the rest of his life.

MIKE: *(To CAROLINE.)* Did you know this was Graeme's wife?

LEO: To Leo Mortimer, everybody!

CAROLINE: *(Angry.)* Oh, for God's sake, Leo, will you please pipe down!

A long silence.

MIKE: *(To LEO.)* This way, Leo... Let's write you out this little cheque, shall we?

LEO follows MIKE out of the kitchen.

A long silence. Only the wind and rain outside. Eventually:

CAROLINE: Mrs Mackie, could I just say that...?

GRAEME: What you doing here?

SALLY: Seems like the end of the world really is here.

CAROLINE: I think, Graeme, your wife is due some form of explanation.

SALLY: It's happening now.

GRAEME: How you find the house?

SALLY Invoice; on your laptop.

CAROLINE: I've been going through a rather difficult period in my life.

GRAEME: I changed the passcode.

SALLY: Greg told me it.

CAROLINE: I suppose one might call it a midlife crisis.

GRAEME: What did I tell you about going near my laptop again!?

SALLY: They've been giving us champagne.

CAROLINE: But if the three of us could find somewhere else to have this conversation then…?

GRAEME: Valium and alcohol, Sally?

SALLY: Not taking my meds.

GRAEME: You what?

CAROLINE: Then that would be…

SALLY: I said I'm not taking them anymore. I wanna stop taking them…

GRAEME: How long since you…?

SALLY: Since this morning.

GRAEME: You can't go cold turkey on…

SALLY: I wanna start feeling life, Graeme. I wanna start *feeling* my life again.

CAROLINE: Then that would be splendid.

GRAEME: *(To CAROLINE.)* She can have these seizures, she…

SALLY: You two ever have sex in here?

CAROLINE: Of course not!

SALLY: We used to have sex in *our* kitchen, Caroline.

GRAEME: *(Grabbing her.)* We're going.

SALLY: But I can't remember the last time he even touched me. Or kissed me on the mouth. Why don't you ever kiss me on the mouth anymore? You can kiss *her* on the mouth, can't you? But you can't kiss *me*. Your own wife. Once upon a time he couldn't stop telling me how beautiful I was. But not now. Cos it's *you* he thinks is beautiful now. It's *you* he thinks is beautiful, it's *you* he thinks is beautiful, it's you, it's you, it's you...

GRAEME goes to grab her again.

Don't you touch me, you whore! You slut!

GRAEME: *(To CAROLINE.)* You're gonna to have to help me.

SALLY: You're a slut, Graeme and a fucking whore!

GRAEME: We need to get her in the van.

SALLY: You still love me, don't you?

GRAEME: You know I do.

SALLY: *(A sudden scream.)* You see? You see? Graeme Mackie belongs to *me,* not you! Graeme Mackie belongs to *me*!!!

CAROLINE: Can we please keep the volume down?

SALLY: Till. Death.

GRAEME: You shouldn't be drinking that.

SALLY: Us. Do. Part.

GRAEME: You know you shouldn't be.

SALLY: Until Death. Until Death.

GRAEME: We need to get you home.

SALLY: I don't wanna go home.

GRAEME: It's where we're gonna go.

SALLY: It's where we're gonna go.

GRAEME: You're gonna put that down and then we're gonna go outside and get into the van and then we're gonna drive home and see the boys.

SALLY: Most of the time he's so lovely to me...

GRAEME: We need to get you home and get you your meds.

SALLY: ...but sometimes he can get very cross.

GRAEME: So put the glass down.

SALLY: Like I'm a naughty child.

GRAEME: You need to put the glass down...

SALLY: Cos I can be a right old handful, can't I?

GRAEME: Please, Sally...

SALLY: And I don't always do as I'm told.

GRAEME: Give me the glass.

SALLY: I'm sometimes a bit...what's the word...unpredictable.

GRAEME: I'm gonna need to call someone.

SALLY: *He* can get out and about but me, I'm stuck at home all day. Cos of our boy. He's not well, you see.

GRAEME: She knows.

SALLY: She knows, she knows, she knows...

GRAEME: That's enough now.

SALLY: So when *he's* all day here fucking you *I'm* all day at home with Greg and he's much bigger than me now and when he gets frustrated he can get very aggressive and...

GRAEME: Sally...

CAROLINE: I'm so sorry...

SALLY: I expect you been looking for this?

SALLY takes out a mobile phone.

GRAEME: Just give it to me,

SALLY: *(Reading from the phone.)* "I need you inside me, Graeme. I want you to make me scream out loud again."

He approaches her and she backs away, struggling to keep on her feet. They circle the central kitchen unit.

GRAEME: Sally!

CAROLINE: I was just drunk.

SALLY: See, he's always had a thing for older women.

GRAEME: For Christ's sake…

SALLY: Probably cos his mum abandoned him when he was little.

GRAEME: I'm gonna lose it in a minute.

SALLY: Ran off with the milkman when he was four years old. Ran off with the bloody milkman.

She starts laughing.

Yeah, and you think it's a joke, don't you? Cos no woman ever *really* runs off with the milkman, do they?

GRAEME: You hear?

SALLY: But *his* did.

CAROLINE: I really think you should let your husband take you home.

SALLY: If he leaves me I don't know what I'll do.

GRAEME: Sally!

SALLY: Probably try and do meself in again.

CAROLINE: Graeme, will you please take her home now!

GRAEME: What you think I'm trying to do?!!

SALLY: But this time, this time I won't make such a dog's dinner of it.

Now LEO re-enters the kitchen.

LEO: Happy days, eh?

CAROLINE: *(To LEO.)* Would you mind giving us a moment?

LEO: Daddykins was charm personified.

CAROLINE: Not now, please!

LEO: Until, that is, I told him about Syria.

He pours himself some bubbly.

However he's still kindly gifted me a rather sizeable cheque.

He produces the cheque as some more glass smashes outside.

CAROLINE: So you're *still* accepting our money, are you?

LEO: I'm sorry?

CAROLINE: I would have thought that went against your fine, upstanding socialistic principles!

LEO: I tell you what.

He slowly rips up the cheque and leaves the pieces on the counter.

GRAEME: Come on, Sall.

LEO: I'm now off outside to kill myself with cigarettes.

SALLY: You mind if I steal one?

LEO: And to watch with enthusiasm the approaching apocalypse.

LEO bows theatrically to SALLY, ushering her off into the garden.

No-one notices her picking up the knife from the top of the play.

GRAEME: Last night you texted me. Said you loved me.

CAROLINE: Look, we can't talk about this now!

GRAEME: *(Holding her passionately.)* Jesus Christ, Caroline, you get right under my skin. You know that? I can't stop thinking about you. The way you talk, the way you move, even the way you smell. It's like I'm out of my mind. I think about you all the time, every minute, of every hour, of every day and it's like a disease!

CAROLINE: My husband is in the next room!

GRAEME: I've been in love with you from the word go. And I never dared say this before as I never believed a woman like you…

CAROLINE: What are they doing out there?

GRAEME: …could ever feel anything for an ordinary bloke like me.

CAROLINE: It's not safe in this weather!

GRAEME: Will you look at me!?

CAROLINE: Graeme, come on…

GRAEME: Sally's like a child to me now. Not a friend, not a wife.

CAROLINE: Your place is with her.

GRAEME: You're my last chance at happiness, Caroline.

CAROLINE: We've both been hugely irresponsible and…

GRAEME: I feel closer to you than I've ever felt to anyone. And I'm offering you my life, I'm offering to leave my family, to move away and live in another country with you like we talked about.

CAROLINE: When did we talk about that ?

GRAEME: We could start again? Away from this broken country, away from all this unhappiness.

CAROLINE: But your family clearly needs you.

GRAEME: You said you loved me and I know you mean it!

CAROLINE: And my family, they need *me*.

GRAEME: I've never been more serious about anything in the whole of my life.

CAROLINE: You love your wife and it's a beautiful, beautiful thing!

GRAEME: I love *you*!

CAROLINE: Graeme, please, understand this: you and I, we could never *ever* be together!

A silence.

GRAEME: Why not?

CAROLINE: Where's that knife?

GRAEME: So it's just been about the sex then?

CAROLINE: My knife was just here and now…

GRAEME: All this time you've just been using me for…

CAROLINE: *(Screaming.)* Oh my God, no!

She rushes out into the garden.

GRAEME: What are you doing here, mate? What the bloody hell are you doing here?

A scream offstage and he rushes out into the storm.

An empty stage for a time.

Then MIKE comes into the kitchen.

MIKE: Caroline?! Did you know anything about this? I give him a cheque for fifty thousand then he tells me he intends to go volunteering in Syria? Is this another thing you've been keeping from me? I didn't put him through Eton and Cambridge for him to bugger off to some warzone and put up tents for a load of bloody refugees!?

He notices Amanda's iPad. Flicks through the images of his wife.

Caroline!

He notices the pieces of his son's ripped up cheque.

Caroline!

He now notices the smoke that's coming out of the oven.

Caroline!

He goes to the oven, opens it. Thick smoke now comes billowing out. He finds a pair of oven gloves. Coughing, he sets down the burnt meat on the units.

Caroline!

The smoke alarm begins to sound loudly.

MIKE stands on the counter and starts waving the oven gloves under the alarm.

Caroline!

He now accidentally kicks the baking tray which causes the joint of meat and the roast potatoes etc to catapult across the kitchen.

Caroline!

Eventually he falls, knocking the golf clubs out across the stage.

The alarm finally stops.

Now AMANDA re-enters the kitchen.

AMANDA: Mr Mortimer?

She goes to him and helps him to his feet.

MIKE: Many thanks.

AMANDA: *(Indicating her iPad.)* I just came back for this.

MIKE: Of course.

AMANDA: I wanted to say I'm really sorry.

MIKE: It's quite alright.

AMANDA: I'm not in a good way. I'm so lonely. So terribly lonely all the time. It's cos I'm missing my mum, you see. I'm really, really missing my mum.

She starts to weep so he goes to her. Puts an arm around her.

MIKE: *(Tenderly.)* It's alright, my darling. I do know how you feel. It's a bugger for us all, isn't it? When we lose our mothers. Even when we lose dreadful mothers like mine.

Now SALLY on, dazed, soaking wet and with blood spatter on her face and clothes.

SALLY: I just did a bad thing.

MIKE: What did she say?

SALLY: I think I just did a very bad thing.

CAROLINE now on, also wet and bloodied, holding the knife towards SALLY.

CAROLINE: You need to step away from my husband.

SALLY: I think maybe I was going to kill him.

CAROLINE: It looked that way.

SALLY: I think maybe I was going to cut out his heart.

LEO on, supporting GRAEME who is bleeding heavily from a knife wound.

MIKE: What going on?

GRAEME now tears off his bloody shirt, sending banknotes flying everywhere. He starts tying the shirt around his wound as a tourniquet.

MIKE on his hands and knees starts gathering up the banknotes on the floor, which is a chaos of notes, blood, red wine, food and golf clubs.

GRAEME: Tie that there, mate. And hold it tight.

LEO helps GRAEME sit.

LEO: *(Doing so.)* Mum, that was the bravest thing I ever saw.

MIKE: For God's sake your money, Graeme! Look at all your money!

CAROLINE: Did you call an ambulance?

LEO: There are none!

CAROLINE: What do you mean?

LEO: There's nothing for forty minutes!

SALLY: I didn't mean to hurt him!

LEO: That's cuts to public services for you!

CAROLINE: This is hardly the time to talk politics, Leo!

SALLY: He's the love of my life.

MIKE: All this brand new money on the floor.

SALLY: What's gonna happen?

GRAEME: Nothing's gonna happen!

SALLY: Please don't let them take me away again!

GRAEME: No-one's ever gonna take you anywhere again.

SALLY: You promise me?

GRAEME: I swear on my life.

SALLY: I'm so sorry, Graeme.

GRAEME: I'm the one who's sorry…

SALLY and GRAEME exit as the storm outside intensifies.

CAROLINE: *(Crying above the storm.)* I don't understand what's happening! It's not meant to be like this? What are we doing to each other? What's wrong with us? What are we always seeking? What more is it that we want? Yes, we've gained the world but lost our souls! We have gained the world but lost our souls!

The storm outside has built to an angry crescendo but now suddenly abates. The wind and rain cease and the kitchen slowly brightens with an immense golden glow. Then a profound stillness in the room.

She drops the knife and then a long silence.

CAROLINE: Mike?

MIKE: Yes, darling?

CAROLINE: We need to start being kinder to each other.

MIKE: I'm sorry?

CAROLINE: We need to start being kind.

A silence.

MIKE: I want you to know that I am so very…

A silence.

LEO: You are so very…?

MIKE: I am so very…

CAROLINE: You are so very…?

LEO: Proud?

A silence.

CAROLINE: And of course I forgive you.

MIKE is now staring straight ahead of himself, in sudden shock.

MIKE: Well, thank God for that.

MIKE now goes into cardiac arrest.

CAROLINE: Mike!

LEO: Dad!

CAROLINE: Mike, what's going on?

LEO: What's happening?

AMANDA: Excuse me, please... I have some experience of this.

AMANDA approaches the gasping man. She starts performing CPR on the stricken man.

This continues for a time.

CAROLINE: Mike!?

LEO: What's happening, Mum?

CAROLINE: Oh God, please, please spare him.

After a time MIKE lies still.

AMANDA: I'm sorry to say, Caroline, your husband is...

LEO: Dad?

AMANDA: ...dead.

LEO: Dad?

CAROLINE: Dead?

AMANDA: Dead.

LEO: *(More desperate.)* Dad?!

CAROLINE: *(Shaking MIKE.)* It's time to wake up, Mike!

LEO: No!!

CAROLINE: It really is time to wake up now!

Now a woman nervously enters the kitchen. Sees the carnage and stands there open-mouthed for a time.

AMANDA: Caroline?

CAROLINE turns towards her.

It seems Mrs Minto is here to view the property.